HANDBOOKS FOR RESEARCH IN POLITICAL BEHAVIOR

edited by James A. Robinson, The Ohio State University

LEGISLATIVE ROLL-CALL ANALYSIS

legislative roll-call analysis

LEE F. ANDERSON
MEREDITH W. WATTS, JR.
ALLEN R. WILCOX

NORTHWESTERN UNIVERSITY PRESS • Evanston • 1966

Second printing, 1968

Copyright © 1966 by Northwestern University Press

Library of Congress Catalog Card Number: 66-13189

Manufactured in the United States of America

EDITOR'S FOREWORD

This is the fourth of a series of handbooks that introduce students to basic techniques for collecting and analyzing political data. The first three volumes describe survey research, content analysis, and data processing. Like its predecessors, this manual on legislative roll-call analysis is intended for the use of undergraduates in the context of classroom instruction and for the individual use of graduate students and faculty members. The series, and this volume especially, aims to involve students directly in analyzing empirical data, in testing hypotheses, and in revising and developing theories about politics. Thanks to recent trends in college and university instruction in the study of government, it is now practicable for undergraduates to obtain personal experience in researching their own questions and problems rather than confining themselves to summaries of the writings of others or to speculation about "what might be the case."

Involving undergraduates in empirical research helps to teach the basis of empirical knowledge and how it is acquired. In an epoch of repeated knowledge explosions, what passes for "conclusions" in one college year may be drastically revised in the next. Although methodologies change also, they are probably less perishable than the results they produce. Hence, one of the most lasting benefits that teachers can give students is an appreciation of research and of its methods.

Legislative roll-call analysis is not, as the authors point out, a new mode of study. The Harvard president and historian A. Lawrence Lowell inaugurated it at the turn of the century, and since then political journals have reported innumerable roll-call studies of parliaments, congresses, assemblies, state legislatures, courts, and city councils. Many topics can be described and analyzed when votes concerning them are recorded. Coalitions, parties, blocs, and groups can be identified. Issues of domestic and foreign policy can be compared and contrasted in terms of proponents and opponents, and "clusters" of votes can be discovered that indicate otherwise hidden philosophic attitudes and governmental actions.

In an era in which legislatures have lost influence to executives, roll-call analysis is a readily available technique for assessing trends and conditions in the "most popular" branch of government. Because roll calls are recorded policy decisions, they constitute a valuable source of policy data that can be correlated with "political process variables," including situations, individual legislators' characteristics (party membership, personality, social background, occupation, previous experience, constituency, *inter alia*), and organizational factors (roles, committee assignments, rules, and procedures). Many current studies of legislatures theorize about decisions and describe how they are made without relating the process of deciding to the outcome or content of decisions. Roll calls can profitably be examined as an important set of "dependent variables," and hypotheses can be tested that relate process variables to policy outcomes.

Messrs. Anderson, Watts, and Wilcox have had much experience, as teachers and as researchers, with roll-call analysis and its many variations. In this book, they review the uses of many indexes that are found in textbooks, monographs, and scientific journals. They also discuss simple indexes now used by journalists and politicians to summarize legislative activities. Readers of this book will therefore find it helpful to them in their roles as citizens and voters as well as in their roles as students and researchers. It is not too much to say that undergraduates who peruse this book will find political theory joined with political practice.

JAMES A. ROBINSON

September, 1965

CONTENTS

LEGISLATIVE ROLL-CALL ANALYSIS

ROLL-CALL VOTES

Legislatures, like other human groups, make decisions in various manners. Voting is one of these decision-making tools. In all modern legislative bodies, some decisions during some phase of the policy process are made and legitimated by means of the vote. The several different voting procedures used by legislative institutions can be grouped into three categories, according to the amount of information each discloses about the positions taken by individual legislators.[1]

Closed or Secret Voting. Completely closed voting is usually applied *only* to cases in which the legislature exercises certain constitutional prerogatives or in which it elects either its own officers or representatives to other bodies.

Semi-Open or Anonymous Voting. Voting of this type is open in the sense that it occurs in the presence of people who have come to listen to speeches. It is closed in the sense that it may not reveal the voting positions of individual legislators. Distinguishable subtypes of anonymous voting are the following, arranged in order of increasing accuracy of the record:

(1) Voting by voice. The chair calls for a voice vote of "yeas" and "nays," then estimates which side has prevailed.
(2) Voting by show of hands.
(3) Voting by standing. Some legislatures elaborate this method by having the "yeas" and "nays" move to opposite sides of the chamber to be counted or by having them move successively in two groups down the center aisle.

Open or Public Voting. In open voting, the individual positions of legislators are recorded. Methods of open voting include the following:

(1) Voting by division. The members divide by "yeas" and "nays," then walk past clerks and tellers who record their names and total the votes.

(2) Voting by roll call. Each member announces his vote as his name is called.

(3) Voting by paper ballot. Members identify themselves and their voting positions on slips of paper. The chair sometimes combines ballot voting with roll-call voting by having each member, as his name is called, mount the rostrum and place his voting slip in a ballot box.

(4) Voting by electronic machine. Members register their votes on a series of buttons located before them. Results are computed and reported immediately.

The third category, public voting, is the concern of this book. We shall refer to all public votes as roll-call votes. Technically, as we have noted, roll-call votes constitute only one subclass of public votes. Because, however, the roll call is the most common type of public vote, the term has come to be associated with all voting procedures that provide a public record of the positions taken by individual legislators.

ROLL-CALL VOTING AS A SUBJECT OF INQUIRY WITHIN POLITICAL SCIENCE

Traditionally, legislatures have been important decision-making structures within modern, democratically organized political systems. When legislatures as institutions are important in the operation of a political system, the behaviors of individuals who occupy roles within the legislature are politically significant and therefore become a subject of inquiry important to political science.

Action on roll calls is one class of legislative behavior that political scientists seek to describe and explain. Interest in roll-call voting dates from the turn of this century. In 1901, A. Lawrence Lowell published a study entitled "The Influence of Party Upon Legislation in England and America."[2] Lowell attempted to use roll-call data to measure the relative influence of party membership in the voting behavior of American and British legislators. Later in the century, Stuart Rice, a pioneer in the advancement of empirical and quantitative research in American political science, further developed roll-call analysis as a method of inquiry. Rice's groundbreaking book, *Quantitative Methods in Politics*, published in 1928, included an extensive discussion of roll-call voting and of methods for quantitatively analyzing roll-call votes.[3]

The work of Lowell and Rice attracted a good deal of attention, but little further research on roll-call voting was done until the 1940's. Following World War II, interest in and research on legislative voting increased significantly among American scholars. Political scientists began to use roll-call data extensively in studying legislatures at the local, state, and national levels of the American political system. In addition, students of international relations and foreign politics have begun to examine public voting in the General Assembly of the United Nations and in foreign legislatures.[4]

The interest in the study of legislative voting that has been manifest during the past two decades results largely from three factors. Recent trends within political science itself consitute one contributing cause. Research has given greater emphasis to analysis of the behavior of individuals acting in political roles rather than to analysis of institutions apart from the behavior of political actors. Moreover, much of political science research has become policy oriented——that is, many political scientists have come to define the task of political analysis as that of accounting for public policy. Furthermore, political science research has become more empirical. Closely related to this is its tendency to become more quantitative.

In light of these developments, it is easy to see why interest in the analysis of legislative voting has increased. To study voting is to study the behavior of individuals acting in political roles. Moreover, since legislators are members of a political elite, to study their behavior is to study behavior that is closely and directly related to the formulation of public policy. Also, the nature of roll-call voting makes empirical analysis comparatively easy. Roll-call votes are "hard" data; also, they are public data. David Truman observes that, "like statistics on elections, they represent discrete acts the fact of whose occurrence is not subject to dispute. They do not depend for their validity as data upon verbal reports of action or upon the impressions of fallible observers."[5]

Most legislative bodies keep public records of the issues on which roll-call votes are taken and of the positions taken by each legislator. The scholar has ready access to these records. Moreover, the nature of roll-call voting facilitates quantitative analysis. The data are already in quantitative form and can easily be collected for purposes of statistical analysis.

Such developments within political science that augment interest in voting behavior have been closely linked to and reinforced by two developments outside political science. Certain new methods of quantitative analysis have proved highly useful in the analysis of roll-call data. Two of the most important of these, Guttman scale analysis and factor analysis, are discussed in subsequent chapters of this book. The advent of high-speed data-processing machines, including computers, also has influenced the development of roll-call analysis. The availability of mechanical and electronic aids has reduced the clerical labor involved in all types of roll-call studies, and, even more importantly, it has permitted the researcher to conduct certain types of analysis that once were impossible.[6]

The net result of the changing orientation within political science combined with the other developments just mentioned has been a rapid growth in research on legislative voting behavior. This book deals with the methods or techniques that political scientists use in such research.

THE PURPOSES OF THIS BOOK

Political scientists study the behavior of political actors in order to expand their understanding of this behavior. The aim of legislative voting research is to understand why legislators vote as they do on roll-calls. To understand or explain behavior one must first be able to describe or characterize it and to measure variations in it. Characterizing and measuring variations in the voting behavior of legislators are not simple. Most legislative bodies have many members, who vote on a large number of roll calls. Several dozen votes of several dozen legislators, examined either one by one or in the aggregate, provide the researcher with little information. Before such a mass of data can yield significant information about a legislative body or about the behaviors of its members, these data must be described in terms of variables that the researcher believes to be meaningful. In their continuing effort to develop ways of characterizing, describing, and measuring variations in the voting behavior of legislators, political scientists have devised or borrowed a variety of methods for processing roll-call data. This book has been written to introduce the beginning student of legislative voting to the most frequently used of these techniques.

WHAT METHODS OF ROLL-CALL ANALYSIS DO

The methods of roll-call analysis, like all tools of inquiry, have no intrinsic worth or merit. Methods derive their value from what they enable us to accomplish. As we have suggested, techniques of roll-call analysis are tools with which to describe or characterize voting behavior in terms of certain variables and to measure variations in this behavior. As such, methods of roll-call analysis are functionally analogous to rulers or scales. We use these devices for describing the variables of height and weight and for measuring variations among objects in terms of the variables. To be more specific, methods of roll-call analysis provide us with means of doing three things:

1. They provide means for describing and measuring variations in the voting behavior of individual legislators.
2. They provide means for describing and measuring variations in the voting behavior of groups of legislators.
3. They provide means for describing and measuring variations among roll calls.

DESCRIBING AND MEASURING VARIATIONS IN THE BEHAVIOR OF INDIVIDUAL LEGISLATORS

The design of many roll-call studies entails an examination of the behavior of individual legislators. In such studies, the researcher attempts to describe the behavior of individuals according to some specified property (variable) and to measure variations among individuals in the degree to which their behaviors evidence this property. For example, a researcher studying the American Congress may believe that the voting behavior of congressmen on certain types of domestic issues can usefully be described as evidencing or lacking "liberalism." "Liberalism" can be thought of as a characteristic of the behavior of legislators. It is assumed that the behavior of legislators will manifest this characteristic in varying degrees. That is, legislators can be arrayed along a continuum ranging from the highly liberal to the highly conservative. The researcher's problem is that of developing from roll-call data an operational definition of "liberalism" and applying this definition to the votes of individual legislators in order to measure variations in the "liberalism" of their voting behavior. Several of the methods of analysis described in this book are designed for dealing with problems of this type.

DESCRIBING AND MEASURING VARIATIONS IN THE BEHAVIOR OF GROUPS OF LEGISLATORS

In contrast to research taking the voting of individual legislators as the unit of analysis, many roll-call studies involve an examination of the voting of groups of legislators. There are two major types of such research. One attempts to describe the behavior of categorically defined groups, and the other seeks to identify blocs or clusters of legislators who regularly vote together.

In the first type of study, the researcher begins with an assemblage of legislators that he designates as a group. Such a group will comprise legislators who share one or more characteristics: for example, the members of a political party; legislators from a certain type of constituency; legislators from a given geographical area; or the members of certain committees. Given the group, the researcher sets out to describe the voting behavior of that group in terms of a specified characteristic and, very likely, to compare its behavior with that of one or more other groups. For instance, a researcher is interested in the leadership of the political parties within a legislature. He believes that the leadership of one of the parties is stronger than the leadership of the other, and he hypothesizes that variations in the strength of party leadership will be reflected in the unity the parties evidence in their voting on roll calls. The researcher predicts that the party which has the stronger leadership will show greater unity than the party which has the weaker leadership. Party unity or cohesion is a characteristic of parties as groups rather than a characteristic of the behaviors of individuals. The researcher's problem is to devise a standard for describing "unity" and to apply this standard to the two parties in order to measure the degree to which they differ.

In the second type of group study, the researcher does not begin with an assemblage of legislators that he treats as a group. Rather, his objective is to identify within a population of legislators those legislators who form voting blocs or groups—that is, those who vote together with some specified regularity. The researcher uses voting data to identify groups of legislators rather than to examine groups defined *a priori*. For example, a researcher believes that the members of a given legislature divide into a number of groups or blocs on roll calls that affect the interests of organized labor. His problem is to determine if this hypothesis is correct—that is, to determine if indeed there are blocs of legislators who regularly vote alike on labor legislation. To do this, the researcher must examine the roll-call votes in a way that will reveal clusters of inter-agreeing legislators if such groups actually exist.

Several of the simpler techniques of analysis discussed in the next few chapters constitute tools that can be used to describe and to measure certain characteristics of the voting behavior of categoric groups. The rather more complex techniques of cluster-bloc analysis, factor analysis, and scale analysis dealt with in later chapters are useful for identifying groups of mutually agreeing legislators.

DESCRIBING AND MEASURING VARIATIONS AMONG ROLL CALLS

Very frequently, research on legislative voting calls for the analysis of votes on a particular class of type of roll call. By class or type is meant a set of roll calls having in common a specified characteristic. In this case, the researcher must select from a total population of roll calls the sample or samples of roll calls that evidence the characteristic specified. Examples would include roll calls on which the level of inter-party disagreement is above a certain point, roll calls on which a given group is highly unified or highly disunified, and roll calls relating to a given substantive issue such as labor relations or foreign aid. Several of the analysis techniques discussed in this handbook can be used to select for analysis those roll calls that evidence some specified common characteristic.

WHAT METHODS OF ROLL-CALL ANALYSIS DO NOT DO

Methods of roll-call analysis, as we have observed, are tools that help the researcher obtain information about the voting behavior of individual legislators, information about the voting behavior of groups of legislators, and information about roll calls. When properly used, these tools are powerful aids of systematic inquiry. By using them, a researcher can do much to illuminate the legislative process and the behaviors of the political actors within this process. But methods of roll-call analysis, like all tools, can be used only for limited purposes. Some things they cannot do. Two of their limitations particularly should be kept in mind when one contemplates or undertakes a study of legislative voting.

In the first place, it should be clearly recognized that techniques of roll-call analysis themselves do not explain to the researcher the patterns he may discern in voting. Techniques of roll-call analysis are, as we noted above, means by which a researcher can process roll-call data in order to discern and to measure patterns of variation in the behaviors of individuals and of groups, but they do not provide information about the factors or variables operating in a situation that explain or account for these variations. Earlier, we compared methods of roll-call analysis to scales or rulers. A ruler will provide information about variations in the height of persons, but it will not provide information about the factors that account for these variations.

Sometimes, the researcher will use information about legislative voting obtained through the application of one or more techniques of analysis as a basis for inferring the "cause" of the patterns observed. He may, for example, observe that a given group of legislators votes together on a set of roll calls involving issues on which the President has taken a stand. He may then infer from his data that these legislators have a common attitude toward the President's program and point to this inferred attitude as the reason for the voting pattern he has observed.

Inference in itself is not illegitimate. Indeed, it is a vital element in systematic inquiry. The researcher should, however, be well aware of the use he makes of inference, and he should state his inferences as explicitly as possible. The theory or data on which inferences are based should be set forth clearly. We shall illustrate the problems of inference at several points throughout the chapters to come.

A second and closely related limitation of roll-call analysis should be kept in mind. Although methods of roll-call analysis provide information about the voting behaviors of legislators, one cannot with confidence infer from information about voting behavior to information about the behavior of legislators in other phases of the legislative process. For example, the fact that a legislator is discerned to vote in a highly partisan way (i.e., he votes regularly with the majority of his own party) does not necessarily indicate anything about the partisanship of his behavior off the floor of the legislative chamber.

> The fact that a legislator is a loyal party man on roll calls does not preclude his being an important agent of pressure groups in introducing bills, his making determined efforts to change a bill in committee to make it more advantageous to the interests of his district, or his attempting to bring about compromises in line with his own personal principles or convictions. . . . A legislator's conduct in the final voting provides little basis for inferences about his behavior at other stages of the legislative process.[7]

THE ORGANIZATION OF THE BOOK

This book is designed to serve the needs of the beginning student of legislative voting. One of its purposes, as indicated above, is to describe the techniques or methods that political scientists most frequently use in analyzing roll-call voting data. In Chapter II, we describe the construction and use of simple indexes as techniques for analyzing the voting behavior of individual legislators. Chapter III discusses the most commonly used methods of measuring the cohesion of categoric groups and of measuring differences between two or more such groups. In Chapter IV, we describe one method by which researchers identify blocs or groups of legislators in agreement. In Chapter V, ways are discussed in which the particular roll calls to be analyzed can be selected from a large number of roll calls. In Chapter VI, we discuss Guttman scale analysis and its application to roll-call data. Chapter VII deals with factor analysis. In the final chapter, we note some of the computer programs that are useful in roll-call analysis.

A NOTE ON DATA PROCESSING

Several of the techniques of analysis described can be executed by hand—that is, without the aid of electronic processing equipment. Other techniques, however, are either impossible or impracticable without the aid of such equipment. Throughout most of the subsequent discussion, therefore, we assume that roll-call data have been put on punch cards and that the researcher will use a computer in processing these data. We do not describe the process of putting roll-call data on punch cards or the general procedures involved in using computers. These are matters discussed in detail in Kenneth Janda's *Data Processing: Applications to Political Research*,[8] to which we refer the reader who is unfamiliar with the use of electronic data-processing equipment and procedures.

A NOTE ON COURT DECISIONS

The discussion of this book is limited to legislative voting. Courts, as well as legislatures, make decisions through voting, and several of the methods described here have been applied in studies of judicial behavior, particularly the behavior of United States Supreme Court justices. Although we shall not discuss these studies, we will note a representative example of the relevant literature. The reader who is interested in judicial decisions should examine the final footnote at the end of the chapters on bloc analysis, Guttman scaling, and factor analysis for examples of judicial studies using these techniques.

NOTES

1 Inter-Parliamentary Union, *Parliaments* (London: Cassell and Company Ltd., 1962), pp. 175-82.
2 American Historical Association, *Annual Report*, 1901.
3 Stuart Rice, *Quantitative Methods in Politics* (New York: Alfred A. Knopf, 1928).
4 References to these studies are found in the footnotes at the end of each chapter.
5 David B. Truman, *The Congressional Party* (New York: John Wiley and Sons, Inc., 1959), p. 12.
6 See Kenneth Janda, *Data Processing: Applications to Political Research* (Evanston, Ill.: Northwestern University Press, 1965) for a discussion of data-processing equipment and its use in political science research.
7 John C. Wahlke, Heinz Eulau, William Buchanan, and LeRoy C. Ferguson, *The Legislative System: Explorations in Legislative Behavior* (New York: John Wiley and Sons, Inc., 1962), p. 239.
8 Janda, *op. cit.*

CHAPTER II METHODS USED IN ANALYZING THE BEHAVIOR OF INDIVIDUAL LEGISLATORS: SIMPLE INDEXES

In Chapter I, we described the techniques that political scientists use in studying legislative voting as tools that provide information about roll calls, about the voting behavior of groups, and about the voting behavior of individual legislators. This chapter is concerned with the latter—the behavior of individual legislators. We shall attempt to describe some simple techniques for describing and measuring variations in the voting behavior of individual legislators.

STEPS IN ANALYZING THE BEHAVIOR OF INDIVIDUAL LEGISLATORS

The analysis of the voting behavior of individual legislators entails three steps. First, the researcher must specify the variable according to which he wishes to describe the legislators' voting behavior. Second, he must develop an instrument for measuring this variable. Third, he must apply this instrument to the voting records of the legislators he studies in order to obtain for each legislator a score or value on the variable being measured.

The first step in this sequence will be dictated by the researcher's theoretical interests and substantive concerns. He will select the variable by which he will describe and measure voting behavior in accordance with the purpose of his research. A great many roll-call studies entail a description of voting in terms of some support-opposition variable. In other words, the type of variable most researchers use in characterizing voting is the legislators' degree of support of or opposition to something, or both.

This "something" might be a group, a policy, or a general ideological position. For example, the researcher may wish to characterize and measure the voting of legislators in terms of support given a political party. Alternatively, he may be interested in describing legislators according to variations in their support for a given policy, e.g., foreign aid. Or he may be interested in analyzing their behavior relative to support given the "liberal" position. In each of these cases, the behavior of legislators is being characterized according to the positions of individuals relative to something.

Once he has selected the variable to be used in describing the voting of legislators, the researcher must develop an instrument for measuring this variable. He must then apply this instrument to the voting records of the legislators being investigated. Students of legislative voting use two principal types of measuring instruments in studying the behavior of individual legislators: indexes and scales. Indexes are the simpler of the two, both to understand and to construct. In this chapter we shall discuss indexes, and in subsequent chapters we shall discuss the construction and use of scales.

THE CONSTRUCTION OF INDEXES

The construction of an index designed to describe and measure the behavior of individuals involves two procedures: the construction of the measuring instrument and the application of the instrument. The first step consists in selecting the roll calls to be used as a measuring instrument. The second entails examining the votes of legislators on the selected roll calls and calculating an index score for each legislator. These procedures can best be described through an examination of two examples of simple index construction.

A researcher believes that the support a legislator gives to his own party is influenced by the competitiveness of the district he represents. Specifically, the researcher hypothesizes that legislators fom districts in which the parties compete closely in elections will be inclined to support their own party less frequently than will legislators from districts that regularly elect members of one party.

The researcher reasons that the concept of "party support" or "party loyalty" is meaningful only in situations in which the legislative parties disagree. An examination of a number of roll calls reveals that on many roll calls the two parties tend to vote similarly. On such roll calls, the researcher reasons, no "party position" exists; hence, votes on these roll calls cannot yield information about the "loyalty" of the legislators to their respective parties. Only roll calls on which some inter-party competition or disagreement occurs will yield information about the relative loyalty of the parties' members.

At this point, the researcher's problem is to operationalize the notion of inter-party disagreement. What behaviors constitute inter-party disagreement? Suppose the investigator concludes that his research purposes are best served by a liberal definition of inter-party competition. He deems that inter-party competition in the voting of legislators exists when one-half or more of the members of one party vote against one-half or more of the members of the other party. This is the researcher's operational definition of inter-party competition.

The researcher now examines the population of roll calls and, using his operational definition, selects from this population the roll calls that meet the specified criterion. Let us say that this examination reveals, in a population of one hundred roll calls, forty roll calls on which fifty per cent or more of the members of one party divide against fifty per cent or more of the members of the other party. These forty roll calls constitute the instrument by which the researcher can now assess legislators in terms of their "party loyalty."

We have now reached the second step in index construction: the application of the measuring instrument. This step is simple. First, the researcher examines each roll call and indicates for each the position taken by the majority of each party. Then, he examines the votes of each legislator on each of the roll calls and indicates whether the legislator voted with or against the majority of his party.

Once this determination is made for each legislator on each roll call, the researcher can summarize his information by giving each legislator an index score that represents the degree of "party loyalty" evidenced by his voting behavior. The index score can be calculated in a number of ways. It can be a simple frequency count—that is, the researcher can indicate for each legislator the number of times (roll calls) he voted with the majority of his own party. In principle, the scores assigned legislators could range between 0 and 40. Alternatively, the researcher may calculate the percentage of times legislators voted with the majority of their party. The base of this percentage can be either the total population of roll calls (40) or the number of roll calls on which a legislator voted. (Roll calls on which a legislator did not vote may be excluded from the calculation.) Another possibility is an index showing a ratio of support to opposition. In such a case, the researcher divides the number (or per cent) of times legislators vote with the majority of their party by the number (per cent) of times they vote against that majority, or vice versa.

Once this task is completed, the researcher has an index of "party loyalty." The index is a measure that discriminates individuals along a continuum ranging from those who voted with their own party most frequently to those who voted with their own party most rarely.[1]

Equipped with this information about the voting behavior of the legislators, the researcher is now ready to examine the hypothesis with which he began. The "party loyalty" of legislators is negatively related to the competitiveness of their districts. The more competitive a district is, the less "party loyalty" legislators will evidence in their roll-call voting. To test the proposition, the researcher could correlate his index of party loyalty with an index of competitiveness. Or he might classify districts into categories according to their competitiveness and then calculate for each category an average or mean index of party loyalty for the legislators falling within the category. He would then examine the difference in the mean indexes of the categories.

Let us look now at a second illustration of index construction. In this instance, the researcher is interested in the relationship between legislators' orientation toward social welfare programs and the competitiveness of their districts. He hypothesizes that the more competitive a district is, the more its representative will support social welfare programs.

In this example, the researcher's task is the same as it was in the first illustration. First, he must construct an instrument by which to assess the variable, "support of welfare programs," and then he must use this instrument to measure variations among legislators in the degree to which their voting evidences the variable.

The instrument will consist of roll calls that relate in some way to social welfare programs. How is the researcher to select from a population of roll calls those that fall into this category? Here we confront an important difference between the first illustration and the second. In constructing an instrument to measure "party loyalty," the researcher had available an objective, quantitative criterion for excluding and including roll calls from his instrument. No such criterion is available in constructing an instrument to measure "support of welfare programs." It is the substance of the roll calls that determines whether they are to be included or excluded from the "social welfare" instrument.

In order to construct his instrument, the researcher must do two things. First, he must specify as completely as he can the meaning of "issues relating to social welfare." He will do this by specifying the boundaries of the category. Next, he must examine his population of roll calls and decide which roll calls fall within these boundaries and which do not. This determination will be simple in many cases, but in others doubt will arise. The researcher must exercise his judgment, and he should realize that he may make one or two types of error. He may include in the category "issues relating to social welfare" roll calls that the legislators voting define as issues involving something other than "social welfare," or he may exclude from the category roll calls that do belong to the category, or he may make both errors. For example, a student of congressional voting finds within the population of roll calls a vote on an amendment to a bill that provides for federal aid to school construction. The amendment is designed to modify the granting procedure in such a way as to prohibit grants to school districts practicing racial segregation in the assignment of children to schools. The researcher might exclude this roll call from his category of "issues relating to social welfare" on the grounds that the roll call deals with civil rights and not with social welfare as such. However, the sponsors of the amendment may have been using the amendment as a tactical means of blocking the federal aid bill, and the legislators may have responded to the amendment as a blocking tactic. If so, the researcher has excluded a roll call from his instrument that in fact belongs within it. Conversely, the researcher might include the roll call on the grounds that it did relate to social welfare when in fact the legislators responded to the vote as an issue in civil rights. If so, the researcher has included a roll call that actually falls outside the category of "issues relating to social welfare."

Some amounts of subjectivity, judgment, and uncertainty enter into virtually all roll-call research in which indexes are used to measure the behavior of legislators on a given type of issue or public policy. This does not mean that the researcher's decision making must be entirely removed from public scrutiny and criticism. The researcher has an obligation to be as explicit as is possible about the rationale he uses in making his choices. He should describe his decision-making process to those who review his research with as much precision, candor, and detail as he commands. Moreover, in the construction of measuring instruments, the researcher need not depend solely on his own judgment. Whenever it is feasible, another investigator should be instructed in the purpose of the research and in the criteria being used in the selection of roll calls, and should then be asked to make an independent selection. The selections of the two researchers can then be checked for reliability. If substantial agreement exists, the researcher can proceed in his analysis with increased confidence in the reliability of his measuring instrument. If the judgments of the two coders diverge significantly, the researcher should reconsider the utility of his criteria. Unreliable instruments can yield reliable information only by accident.

Let us now return to the illustration and complete the example. After the researcher has selected the roll calls that will compose his instrument, he must convert "yea" and "nay" votes into positive and negative responses—that is, he must determine for each roll call whether a "yea" or a "nay" vote constitutes a vote in support of or in opposition to welfare programs. He then examines the voting record of each legislator on the selected roll calls and, as in the case of the first illustration, converts this information into an index score for each legislator.

SOME EXAMPLES OF INDEXES USED IN THE STUDY OF CONGRESSIONAL VOTING

We have described in some detail the process of index construction. The types of variable that can be measured by means of indexes are not limited so long as the researcher is able to devise a satisfactory measuring instrument. In order to illustrate the range of variables that can be examined, we will describe briefly a few indexes that are used in studies of Congressional voting.

The *Congressional Quarterly*[2] has developed several indexes that it reports for each session of the Congress. Students of Congressional voting can sometimes make direct use of the *Congressional Quarterly* indexes, thereby avoiding the chore of constructing their own.[3] These indexes may suggest to students of other legislatures the types of measures they wish to develop in their own research.

Indexes of Presidential Support and Opposition. CQ identifies the roll calls occuring on issues on which the President has taken a position. Using these roll calls as its instrument, CQ measures congressmen according to their degree of support of and opposition to the President's program. This index is expressed as the percentage of times each congressman voted in support of the President's position and the percentage of times each congressman voted in opposition to the President's position.

Indexes of Party Support and Opposition. These indexes are similar to the index of party loyalty discussed in the illustration above. They note the percentage of times a congressman voted with and the percentage of times he voted against the majority of his own party on roll calls on which one-half or more of the members of one party opposed one-half or more of the members of the other party.

Bipartisan Voting Scores. These scores give the percentage of times a member voted in agreement or disagreement with the majority position when majorities of both parties assumed the same position on a measure.

Federal Role Scores. Federal role scores show the percentage of times a member supported or opposed measures involving expansion of the federal government's role in the society, e.g., in public housing, aid to education, or minimum wage scale.

Conservative Coalition Scores. These scores give the percentage of times a member supported or opposed the stand of Republicans and Southern Democrats when a majority of Republicans joined by a majority of Southern Democrats opposed a majority of Northern Democrats.

Interest groups and journals of opinion sometimes construct indexes designed to measure variations in the behavior of legislators on roll calls of particular interest to them. Perhaps the best known and most widely used of these are the indexes constructed by *The New Republic* magazine at the conclusion of each Congress. The editors of the magazine select from votes taken in each house certain roll calls (for the most part roll calls on major domestic issues) and then indicate approval or disapproval of each senator's and congressman's vote on each of the selected roll calls. Students of American politics interested in the general liberal-conservative disposition of congressmen have been able to make a good deal of use of the *New Republic's* indexes either directly or after subjecting them to slight modifications.[4]

More Complex Indexes. We have been discussing very simple forms of indexes. More elaborate types may be constructed. For example, it is possible to treat the responses of legislators in more complex ways than we have done in our illustrations. David Truman, in a study of the Senate and the House of Representatives during the 81st Congress, provides examples of indexes involving a more complex coding and scoring system.[5] Truman constructs and uses an Index of Administration Support and an Index of Party Orthodoxy. The congressmen's responses to the roll calls included in each index are scored by five categories. These are:

5 = voted for
4 = paired for
3 = no vote
2 = paired against
1 = voted against

Truman then averages the legislators' scores to obtain an overall index score.

Truman's major assumption is that voting may lie on a continuum of intensity that can be ranged from one to five. The extreme scores (1 and 5) indicate a more intense feeling about the issue than any of the midpoints. The "no vote" category is taken to indicate indifference to the issue rather than any other reason for absence during a roll call (e.g., attendance at a committee meeting, illness, junket to Europe).[6]

Another type of complex index is one in which two simple indexes are combined to produce a third. Donald Matthews uses such an index in his study of United States senators.[7] Matthews constructs (from *New Republic* data) an Index of Conservatism-Liberalism to measure variations among the senators in respect to ideology. Further, he measures variations among the senators in respect to party support, using as an index the *Congressional Quarterly* party unity scores. Matthews then relates these two indexes to one another in order to produce a measure that he terms an Index of Party Effort. He reasoned that "while a senator's party regularity is largely a function of his ideological position, it is not entirely determined by this factor."[8] In short, party membership is believed to be a variable factor exerting influence on senators' voting independent of the effects of ideological position. The Index of Party Effort is designed as a means of assessing the independent effect of party.

Matthews describes the way in which the index was constructed as follows:

> The index of party effort was computed in the following manner. First, a scatter diagram was made for each Congress and each party, plotting the senators' conservatism-liberalism scores along the "x" axis and party-unity scores along the "y" axis. Then the equation of the line of regression was computed. Since the senators' conservatism-liberalism scores

were known it was then a simple matter to determine from the equation what their party-unity score would be if they were normal partisans.[9] The difference between a senator's expected party score and his actual score (the distance between his position on the scatter diagram and the line of regression) is his index of party effort. All senators whose actual party-unity scores were four points or more higher than expected were classified as having high party-effort scores; those whose actual party-unity scores were within three points of the expected value were classified as having average indices of party effort; those whose party-unity scores were four points or more below the expected value were classified as having low party-effort scores.[10]

TWO ILLUSTRATIONS OF THE USE OF SIMPLE INDEXES[11]

American political parties are often characterized as loose alliances of shifting interests that display little or no stable difference in their orientation toward issues of public policy. Is this correct, or are there discernible policy-oriented differences between the parties? One way to answer this question partially is to examine the voting records of the parties' congressional members. We might hypothesize that such an examination will reveal that the parties tend to diverge from one another even though some members of each party vote with the opposition as frequently as they do with the majority of their own party. Simple indexes can be used to examine this hypothesis. Truman's Index of Administration Support, mentioned above, provides one illustration.

Figure II-1 shows the distribution of senators in the 81st Congress, second session, by level of Administration support.[12] (The lower the score, the less support was given Administration policies.) This array of scores and legislators reveals much about the relationship between the two parties and about the internal voting structure of each party. The distribution clearly shows that both parties comprise members who vary considerably in their support of Administration programs. The distribution also indicates that "the center of gravity of the two parties were not only distinguishable but consistently different."[13] The score of the most anti-Administration Democrat (Senator Byrd of Virginia) equaled the model Republican score. Conversely, Senator

Smith of New Jersey, a Republican, supported the Administration nearly as frequently as did the most characteristic of Democratic senators.

FIGURE II-1

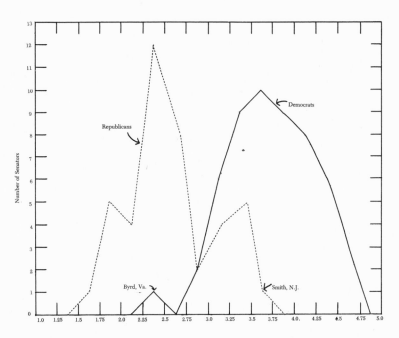

Mean Administration Support Indexes

Inter-party differences: distribution of Republicans and Democratic senators according to mean Administration support indexes, 81st Congress, second session.

At several points in the discussion, we have used as illustration hypothetical research that involved the relating of constituency characteristics (e.g., degree of inter-party competition) to some aspect of legislators' voting behavior as measured by an index. This type of analysis is illustrated by research relating variations in voting behavior to variations in the urbanization of legislators' constituencies. V. O. Key provided an example of such an analysis.[14] Key used an index of conservatism-liberalism constructed by the *New Republic* from roll calls in the House of Representatives during the 1956 session of the Congress to characterize the legislators' voting. (This ranks congressmen on a ten-point scale ranging from 0, the most conservative, to 10, the most liberal.) Then, using a classification scheme provided by the *Congressional Quarterly*, Key grouped congressional districts into four types:

District Type	Description
I	Primarily rural districts, having no city of more than 25,000.
II	Small-town districts, having no city of more than 50,000.
III	Mid-urban districts, "substantially influenced" by a city of from 50,000 to 200,000.
IV	Metropolitan districts, with cities of 200,000 or over or within such cities.

Key then related type of district to index scores. This he did by calculating for the Republicans the percentage of legislators with a score of 4 or more in each of the four types of districts and by calculating for the non-Southern Democrats the percentage of legislators with a score of 8 or more in each type. The resulting information is summarized in Table II-1.

TABLE II-1

Republicans

District Type	Per Cent of Representatives with Score of 4 or More
I	22%
II	24%
III	43%
IV	57%

Non-Southern Democrats

District Type	Per Cent of Representatives with Score of 8 or more
I	59%
II	59%
III	81%
IV	90%

In both cases, we observe the expected relationship. The proportion of "liberal" legislators tends to increase progressively at each level of urbanization.

WEAKNESSES OF INDEXES

A great deal of roll-call research makes fruitful use of indexes in measuring variations in the voting behavior of individual legislators. As measuring instruments, nevertheless, indexes, have certain weaknesses.[15] If an instrument is to give maximally reliable and valid information about a behavior, the instrument must be unidimensional: It must measure a single variable. For example, the researcher interested in measuring variations among legislators in their "support of welfare programs" needs an instrument that will measure this and only this variable. As we have indicated in discussing the construction of an index to measure "support of welfare programs," the researcher's judgment can err in the inclusion and exclusion of roll calls from the instrument. Nothing in the procedure of index construction provides an external check on the validity of the researcher's judgment. It is quite possible to construct an instrument that includes roll calls to which voting responses do not reflect the variable the researcher is trying to measure. Such an instrument is not a pure measure of the variable. The situation is rather like that which would result if individuals were examined with a scale that sometimes measured their height, sometimes measured their girth, and sometimes measured the color of their hair. The scale would yield a single score for each individual, but the score's meaning would be highly dubious.

There is no way to construct from roll-call data measuring instruments of unquestionable unidimensionality. Confidence in instruments can be enhanced, however, if the researcher's judgment can be supplemented by empirical tests of unidimensionality. One of the principal merits of scaling, which we shall discuss in later chapters, is that it provides such empirical tests.

NOTES

[1] See Julius Turner, *Party and Constituency* (Baltimore: Johns Hopkins Press, 1951) for an example of the use of such an index. For a

critical discussion of the index as a measure of the concept of party loyalty, see C. O. Smith and G. L. Field, "The Responsibility of Parties in Congress: Myth and Reality," *Southwestern Social Science Quarterly,* 34 (June, 1953), 33ff.

2 The Congressional Quarterly Service, 1735 K Street, N. W., Washington, D. C. The measures discussed have been developed in various forms since 1946. See especially the *Quarterly's* periodic *Almanac.*

3 For examples of the use of *CQ* indexes see Lewis A. Froman, Jr., *Congressmen and Their Constituencies* (Chicago: Rand McNally & Co., 1963), especially Part II, "Constituency Influences on Congressmen." Some of this material also appears in Lewis A. Froman, Jr., "Inter-Party Constituency Differences and Congressional Voting Behavior," *American Political Science Review,* 57 (March, 1963), 57-61.

4 For examples of the use of *New Republic* indexes see Donald R. Matthews, *U.S. Senators and Their World* (Chapel Hill: The University of North Carolina Press, 1960), pp. 276-78; D. R. Brimhall and A. S. Otis, "Consistency in Congressional Voting," *Journal of Applied Psychology,* 32 (February, 1948), 1-15; N. L. Gage and B. Shimberg, "Measuring Senatorial 'Progressivism,'" *Journal of Abnormal and Social Psychology,* 44 (January, 1944), 112-17.

5 David B. Truman, *The Congressional Party: A Case Study* (New York: John Wiley and Sons, Inc., 1959).

6 For a discussion of the two indexes and their construction, see Truman, *op. cit.,* pp. 326-29.

7 Matthews, *op. cit.*

8 *Ibid.,* p. 135.

9 For a discussion of scatter diagrams and lines of regressions, see any standard textbook in statistics. One discussion can be found in V. O. Key, *A Primer of Statistics for Political Scientists* (New York: Thomas Y. Crowell Co., 1954), pp. 74ff.

10Matthews, *op. cit.,* p. 280.

11Other illustrations include the writings cited in notes 3 and 4. See also S. P. Huntington, "A Revised Theory of American Party Politics," *American Political Science Review,* 54 (September, 1950), 669-77; and Julius Turner, *op. cit.*

12Truman, *op. cit.,* p. 284.

13Truman, p. 285.

14V. O. Key, *Public Opinion and American Democracy* (New York: Alfred A. Knopf, 1961), pp. 283-86.

15For a critical discussion of indexes, see Duncan MacRae, Jr., *Dimensions of Congressional Voting* (Berkeley: University of California Press, 1958), pp. 300-308.

CHAPTER III   **METHODS USED IN ANALYZING**
THE BEHAVIOR OF CATEGORIC
GROUPS

In addition to studying the behavior of individual legislators, political scientists frequently examine the behavior of groups of legislators. In Chapter I, we indicated that two types of groups can be studied. We termed one of these types empirical groups and defined them as clusters or blocs of legislators who regularly vote together. We termed the second type categoric groups and defined them as collections of legislators grouped into categories by the researcher on the basis of one or more commonly shared characteristics.

In this chapter, we shall discuss categoric groups. First we shall indicate some of the types of categoric groups that roll-call voting studies analyze. We shall then describe some of the methods of analysis that political scientists use in their efforts to describe and to measure the behavior of these groups.

SOME TYPICAL CATEGORIC GROUPS

The distinguishing mark of research on the voting behavior of categoric groups is that the analysis begins with the classification of legislators into certain categories or groups. These categories originate in the mind of the researcher and, presumably, will be related to his theoretical concerns and substantive interests. The number of ways in which legislators may be classified or grouped has no established limit; however, certain generic classifications are found repeatedly in most of the literature on legislative behavior. The most common bases for these classifications are *political party, regional background, constituency type,* and *per-*

sonal characteristics. These categories are not mutually independent, and it is likely that they will be interrelated in any given analysis. Nevertheless, each invokes a slightly different criterion for placing legislators in groups, and it is possible to separate them conceptually.

In the first category, the critical criterion is the political party affiliation of the legislator. This is, of course, the most conspicuous label to pin on a representative, because the members of most of the legislatures in the American society are elected on a partisan basis. It is assumed that members will respond in some way to their partisan affiliation and that knowledge of that affiliation will shed some light on the representative's responses to roll-call votes. Although the effects of party may vary considerably with the political and cultural setting of any given legislative body, the general salience of the concept *party* in American political life makes it an obvious point of departure for legislative analysis.[1]

In the second general category, the *regional* association of the legislators is taken as a defining category. The nature of the distinction that a researcher will invoke will vary with the setting of the legislature, but geographical distribution will generally provide the criterion for regional association. Common distinctions are those made between North and South, East and West, upstate and downstate, central city and suburbs, or metropolitan area and "outstate" constituencies.[2]

The third type of categorization is based on the assumption that the *nature of the legislator's constituency* will affect his response to roll-call voting. The criterion is not necessarily geographical in this case, because the constituency characteristics that the researcher wants to investigate may not conform to simple geographical demarcations. Here the researcher is interested in the social, economic, or political characteristics of the legislator's home district, or all three. Numerous studies of the conflict between rural and urban constituencies differentiate by farm population or by degree of urbanization.[3] Other investigators have grouped legislators according to the socio-economic status (SES) of their constituencies.[4] The ethnicity (e.g., percentage of foreign-born population) or means of economic subsistence (e.g., manufacturing, cotton production, steel, milk production) of a district can be used also as defining categories. Degree of inter-party competition is the most common political characteristic used in categorizing legislators.[5]

The *personal characteristics* of the individual legislator also may be considered relevant to the study. Some research has been done on "personality" variables, such as the need for esteem and the drive for power,[6] but the more common categories usually deal with less recondite concepts—for example, *tenure* in the legislature, *occupation, age, sex, committee assignment,* and *leadership position.*[7]

TYPES OF VARIABLES USED IN ANALYZING CATEGORIC GROUPS

Once the researcher has grouped legislators in one or more categories, his next task is to analyze the voting of these groups on the roll calls he has selected for study. This analysis consists in describing and measuring the groups' voting behavior in terms of certain characteristics or variables. These characteristics, like the categories used in defining groups, originate with the researcher. The variables that may be used in describing voting behaviors are not limited so long as the researcher can devise a means of measuring the variables.

Two particular types of variables are most frequently used in analyzing categoric groups. One of these is internal cohesion, or the unity that groups display in their voting. The other is the degree to which the behavior of a given group differs from the behavior of one or more other groups. In the last several years, political scientists have either developed or borrowed several techniques for measuring intra-group cohesion and inter-group difference. In the remainder of this chapter, we shall describe several of these measures.

MEASURES OF INTRA-GROUP COHESION

The researcher has available many techniques for assessing intra-group cohesion or solidarity. For the purposes of this discussion, these can be divided into two types. The first and most simple type of measure comprises indexes of cohesion based on the percentage distribution of "yea" and "nay" votes on an issue. The second type consists of indexes of cohesion based on the frequency of interpersonal agreement among the members of a group.

INDEXES OF COHESION

The best known and most widely used measure of intra-group cohesion is the Rice Index of Cohesion. Other and somewhat less frequently used measures are the index of "absolute cohesion" and the index of "relative cohesion." The derivations of both these indexes are similar to that of the Rice index, but for various reasons they stress slightly different characteristics of a group's voting structure.

Rice Index of Cohesion. This measure of cohesion was first proposed by the sociologist Stuart A. Rice in the 1920's.[8] The impetus for its development was Rice's desire to describe the behavior of legislative groups at the roll-call voting stage and to facilitate the quantitative comparison of behavior across groups. In particular, Rice focused on the concept of cohesion as it could be detected in categorically defined subgroups within a legislature.

For the purposes of the index, Rice defined cohesion as the extent to which the distribution of votes on a legislative roll call deviates from the distribution that would be expected if all influences operated in a random fashion. The argument states that, if one hundred votes were cast in a purely random manner, they would distribute themselves equally on both sides of the issue, i.e., fifty "yeas" to fifty "nays." This instance is defined as the case of minimum cohesion and is assigned the index value of zero. The opposite extreme occurs when all members vote on the same side of an issue—that is considered complete cohesion and is assigned the index value of 100. The index is thus established as having a range from 0 to 100.

Intermediate values in this range are determined by the degree to which the percentage of "yea" votes deviates from 50.0

in either direction, toward 0.0 or toward 100.0. For example, when 75 percent vote "yea" on an issue, there is a 25/50 or 50-per-cent departure from zero cohesion toward complete cohesion; the index is 50.0.

Computationally, the index may be derived by converting the number of "yeas" and "nays" into percentages of the total number of group members voting. The Rice index is then expressed as the absolute difference between the two percentage figures. Consider the following votes from the 1961 session of the U.S. Senate (identification numbers are arbitrarily assigned for this illustration and for those that follow):

On sample roll call 1, the Democrats voted 32 for and 31 against (total, 63). The Republicans split 18 for and 15 against (total, 33).

Democrats:
   Per cent for = 32/63 × 100.0 = 50.8.
   Per cent against = 31/63 × 100.0 = 49.2.
   Rice index = 50.8 — 49.2 = 1.6.

Republicans:
   Per cent for = 18/33 × 100.0 = 54.5.
   Per cent against = 15/33 × 100.0 = 45.4.
   Rice index = 54.5 — 45.4 = 9.1.

On the second sample roll call, the Democrats voted 48 for and eight against (total, 56). The Republicans voted 19 for and ten against (total, 29). Note that party majorities were not aligned against one another on this issue.

Democrats:
   Per cent for = 48/56 × 100.0 = 85.7.
   Per cent against = 8/56 × 100.0 = 14.3.
   Rice index = 85.7 — 14.3 = 71.4.

Republicans:
   Per cent for = 19/29 × 100.0 = 65.5.
   Per cent against = 10/29 × 100.0 = 34.5.
   Rice index = 65.5 — 34.5 = 31.0.

On the third sample roll-call vote, opposing majorities confronted each other, with the Democrats voting three for and

57 against (total, 60). The Republican delegation voted 29 for
and four against (total, 33).

Democrats:
Per cent for $= 3/60 \times 100.0 = 5.0$.
Per cent against $= 57/60 \times 100.0 = 95.0$.
Rice index $= 95.0 - 5.0 = 90.0$.

(Note that, since the *absolute* difference between the two
percentage figures is wanted, the smaller percentage is always
subtracted from the larger.)

Republicans:
Per cent for $= 29/33 \times 100.0 = 87.9$.
Per cent against $= 4/33 \times 100.0 = 12.1$.
Rice index $= 87.9 - 12.1 = 75.8$.

Using the Rice indexes of cohesion to compare the response of
the party delegations on the three issues, we can see that the first
issue did not elicit a party-oriented response. Both parties split
about equally, and both had very low index values.

Majorities of both parties favored the second issue. Thus,
there was some cohesion *within* parties on the measure, but
there was also agreement *between* parties.

On the third roll-call vote, sizable majorities opposed each
other. The Democrats were more cohesive in their response
opposing the bill (index $= 90$) than the Republicans were in
their favorable response (index $= 75.8$).

It is possible also to find the index of cohesion for a set of
legislative roll calls by taking the average of the Rice indexes
computed for each roll call in the set. For the three examples
given above, we find that the Democrats voted together with an
average cohesion of

$$\frac{1.6 + 71.4 + 90.0}{3} = 54.3$$

The Republicans were less successful in maintaining cohesion
and achieved an average index of

$$\frac{9.1 + 31.0 + 75.8}{3} = 38.6$$

Average indexes such as these may be useful in assessing the cohesion of categoric groups on a large number of issues that arise during the legislative session. However, it is not generally advisable simply to aggregate numerical indexes without having some idea of the issues that are involved. A knowledge of the content of the roll calls is a useful guard against the possibility of mistaken inference, and it is almost mandatory if one wishes to determine the types of issue that elicit the greatest measure of group cohesion. A common technique for testing the differential effects of group identification on voting response is dividing the roll calls into issue areas, e.g., foreign policy, farm supports, civil rights, and the like. It is then possible to determine which issues generally inspire unity of response.[9]

In these examples, political parties constituted the categoric groups whose cohesion is measured. Any categoric group can be treated in the same manner.[10] For example, one might use the method to compare the cohesion of the Chicago delegation in the Illinois Assembly with the cohesion of the downstate delegates.

The Index of Absolute Cohesion. This index also provides a measure of intra-group solidarity. The index expresses the party majority on a roll call as a percentage of the *total* possible voting members in the group, regardless how many were actually present at the vote count. Therefore, if 100 Republicans are in the legislature and 75 vote "yea" on an issue, the index of absolute cohesion is 75 per cent. The disposition of the other 25 votes is irrelevant; the index would have the same value if the remaining members were present and voting "nay" or if they were absent altogether. As its author argues, "this test retains the simplicity of a single, easily understood expression useful in identification of groups in conflict without adding the bi-dimensionality of intra-group cohesion."[11] In other words, this measure is meant to estimate unity without considering the extent of disunity that might exist in the group.

Using the three roll calls from the previous illustration, we find that the total Democratic membership was 64, while the Republicans had 36 members in the Senate. The indexes of absolute cohesion are calculated as follows:

Roll Call 1 (Democrats 32-31, Republicans 18-15):
  Democrats' index = 32/64 × 100.0 = 50.0%.
  Republicans' index = 18/36 × 100.0 = 50.0%.
Roll Call 2 (Democrats 48-8, Republicans 19-10):
  Democrats' index = 48/64 × 100.0 = 75.0%.
  Republicans' index = 19/36 × 100.0 = 52.8%.
Roll Call 3 (Democrats 3-57, Republicans 29-4):
  Democrats' index = 57/64 × 100.0 = 89.1%.
  Republicans' index = 29/36 × 100.0 = 80.6%.

As in the Rice index procedure, each absolute-cohesion index applies to a single roll-call vote. If an aggregate measure is desired for a set of roll calls, the average index can be calculated by adding the values of the index for each roll call and dividing the result by the number of roll calls.

The Index of Relative Cohesion. The index of relative cohesion is similar to the index of absolute cohesion except that it takes into account the number of absences on each roll call. The index value expresses the number in the group majority as a percentage of members of the group who vote on the measure. All those in the group who are not present at the voting stage, or who otherwise abstain, are deleted from the calculation.

For the sample of roll calls considered above, the relative cohesion indexes are:

Roll Call 1 (Democrats 32-31, Republicans 18-15):
  Democrats' index = 32/63 × 100.0 = 50.8%.
  Republicans' index = 18/33 × 100.0 = 54.5%.
Roll Call 2 (Democrats 48-8, Republicans 19-10):
  Democrats' index = 48/56 × 100.0 = 85.7%.
  Republicans' index = 19/29 × 100.0 = 65.5%.
Roll Call 3 (Democrats 3-57, Republicans 29-4):
  Democrats' index = 57/60 × 100.0 = 95.0%.
  Republicans' index = 29/33 × 100.0 = 87.9%.

COMPARISON OF THE THREE INDEXES OF COHESION

Table III-1 presents the indexes calculated in the examples above. Two additional roll calls have been added to amplify the general relationship among the Rice index of cohesion and the indexes of absolute and relative cohesion.

It can be seen that a simple mathematical relationship obtains between the Rice measure and the index of relative cohesion. The former may easily be derived from the latter by subtracting the minority percentage from the relative-cohesion index (e.g., Roll Call 1: $1.6 = 50.8 - [100.0 - 50.8] = 50.8 - 49.2$). The absolute-cohesion index, however, has no simple or necessary relationship to either of the others because its percentages are computed on a different base.

A minimum of divergence among the three indexes is evident in cases in which nearly all members are present and voting. The greater the number of members missing, the more the absolute-cohesion index will diverge from the other two. This drawback of the absolute index can be serious if one wishes to take abstentions or absences into account; it would be wiser in such a case to use one of the other indexes.

TABLE III-1

COMPARISON OF THREE INDEXES OF COHESION
ON FIVE SELECTED ROLL CALLS

Roll Call	Yeas	Nays	Rice Index	Relative Index	Absolute Index
1					
D	32	31	1.6	50.8	50.0
R	18	15	9.1	54.5	50.0
2					
D	48	8	71.4	85.7	75.0
R	19	10	31.0	65.5	52.8
3					
D	3	57	90.0	95.0	89.1
R	29	4	75.8	87.9	80.6
4					
D	60	0	100.0	100.0	93.6
R	32	0	100.0	100.0	88.9
5					
D	14	47	54.1	77.0	73.4
R	16	17	3.0	51.5	47.2

Another point of comparison among the three indexes concerns the minimum and maximum values that they can obtain. In the Rice index, the values can vary between 0.0 and 100.0 no matter how many members are present and voting. The size of the voting group at any one time is irrelevant to the index and plays no part in the value it can obtain.

The index of absolute cohesion can fall to 0.0 only if no one from a particular delegation votes on a measure. It can attain a value of 100.0 only if all members are present and voting together.

The index of relative cohesion can never fall below 50.0, but it can reach 100.0 at any time that all members voting agree on the issue.

In choosing among these three indexes, it should be remembered that the Rice measure incorporates the concept of conflict as well as that of cohesion. The relative-cohesion measure can include this dimension only when it is converted to the Rice value. If consideration of cohesion as a bi-dimensional phenomenon is theoretically important then use of the more popular Rice index is advisable.

An added advantage of the Rice index is simply that it is commonly known and understood because of its extensive use in writings on legislative behavior. Because the Rice index has been used much more widely than the other two measures, the researcher will be better able to relate his findings to other studies if he uses it.

THE PROBLEM OF INFERENCE FROM AN INDEX OF COHESION

When an investigator undertakes to gauge the cohesion of a group he is studying—whether it be a political party, sectional delegation, or occupational group—he may be tempted to infer that the basis for categorization is the *cause* of the cohesion he finds. For example, if he finds that each party in the legislature is highly cohesive on a set of issues, he may conclude that party affiliation is the cause of cohesion; or, if all Southern senators exhibit high cohesion on particular bills, he may cite similarity of sectional background as the *cause* of intra-group solidarity. In general, this has been the (sometimes implicit) assumption of many studies that have incorporated the concept of cohesion.[12] And it is clear that much work done on intra-group voting cohesion must make such assumptions in order to link legislative voting patterns to other relevant variables. However, some of the difficulties inherent in this procedure should be noted.

In the first place, the "selection variable" (party, constituency type, region) may not actually be the most important influence affecting the cohesiveness of the legislative groups studied. Other variables may have an important impact on cohesion but may not be included in the analysis. For example, Democrats in a state legislature may tend to vote with a high degree of cohesion on social-welfare issues. But it may also be true that most of the Democrats come from low-SES urban constituencies. In this case, the nature of the constituency may be the crucial variable promoting similarity of voting response. One would test this hypothesis by analyzing the behavior of Democrats from high-SES districts and that of Republicans from low-SES districts. If the constituency hypothesis holds, one would expect to find Democrats from wealthy districts deviating from the party vote and Republicans from a poorer area agreeing with the pro-welfare Democrats.

Also, party-constituency interaction may be further complicated by the addition of new variables. Occupation of the legislator, his conception of constituency demands, his conception of the role he plays as a representative of the people,[13] his position in the leadership hierarchy of the party and legislature,[14] and the particular nature of the issues studied may all wield considerable influence at various stages of the voting process. It is incumbent on the researcher to be aware of such possible interactions among variables and to attempt to assess the conditions under which they may operate.[15]

The user of cohesion indexes should be cautioned also that a particular index may occur by chance. Since no statistical test of significance has been developed to determine the probability that the cohesion exhibited by a group may be purely accidental, the researcher must be prepared to absorb the ambiguity in the index itself. If he cannot draw on supplementary data to substantiate his interpretations, he should at least analyze enough roll calls to assure himself that the pattern occurs with some consistency.

INDEXES OF INTRA-GROUP COHESION BASED ON
MEASURES OF INTERPERSONAL AGREEMENT

The simple indexes of cohesion just described are based on the distribution of "yea" and "nay" votes within a group on single roll calls. Cohesion is thus treated as a function of the relative numerical size of the factions within a group. An alternative way in which to conceptualize cohesion is to view it as a characteristic of the interpersonal relations of the group's members. The more frequently the group members agree with one another, the more cohesive the group is.

Measures of Interpersonal Agreement. The simplest measure of interpersonal agreement is the number of times two given legislators agree on a series of roll calls. As might be expected, the procedure is to isolate the set of roll calls that is of interest to the researcher and to calculate the number of roll calls on which each pair of legislators agrees. A simple notation for this method is: IA (Index of Agreement) $= f$; f is the number of roll-call votes on which both legislators responded similarly. Thus, if legislators 1 and 2 voted alike on 75 roll calls, $IA_{12} = 75$.[16]

The obvious objection to this procedure is that the index in no way indicates the total number of roll calls included in the set. If the same number of roll calls is used in calculating all IA's (IA_{12}, IA_{13}, . . .), no difficulty occurs, and the indexes will be comparable from one pair of legislators to another. But, when legislators differ in their rates of absenteeism, the total number of *possible* agreements will vary considerably from one pair to another. Therefore, it may be desirable to express the index as a function of the total number of possible agreements—that is, as an adjusted figure with varying set sizes. A possible notation for this correction factor is: $IA = (f/t) \times 100$, where f is the total number of agreements, and t is the total number of roll calls in the set on which both legislators voted. The theory behind this formulation is that some members may not appear on the floor of the legislature during a roll call and that this varying rate of absenteeism should not be allowed to reduce the agreement index. It is possible, for example, that a legislator might be ill or in committee hearings and thereby miss several votes; but his absence would reduce the value of his agreement indexes, which would then underestimate his tendency to vote with certain members. Using this modified formula for the index, we would calculate *IA* as a percentage of *possible* mutual responses, even though each pair of legislators would share a slightly different set size.

A further alteration in indexing agreement has been made by Arend Lijphart for the special problem of United Nations voting.[17] In that assemblage, it is common for a national delegation to abstain deliberately from voting, even though the delegation may be present at the meetings. The abstention itself has a substantive meaning, and the qualitative interpretation of this response can generally be specified more clearly than a "no vote" on the floor of, say, the United States Congress. Lijphart proposes that an abstention be coded as a "partial agreement," since it may, he suggests, be a deliberate "no vote" to avoid disagreement with certain other nations. If his assumption is valid, we can interpret an abstention as a partial agreement with both sides of the issue. The formula would be:

$$IA = \frac{f - \frac{1}{2}g}{t} \times 100\%$$

where

f is the number of votes on which A and B agreed completely,

g is the number of votes on which A and B agreed partially, and

t is the total number of votes in which *both* A and B participate.[18]

Observers of the United Nations (and other voting groups to which the modified *IA* might be applied) will have to settle the substantive issue at stake here. Whether an abstention can qualify as a "partial agreement" may vary considerably from one issue to another, and it is probably wise to be cautious in assuming that it can. On the other hand, certain assumptions must be made in the use of either of the other *IA* formulas; but no formula should be used uncritically. Since much of statistics and measurement is based on approximations, the researcher should not be unduly reticent about making use of available quantitative techniques. Rather, he should state his assumptions carefully and should relate them to the specific requirements of the data he has at hand when he reports the results of his research.

Once the index of agreement for each pair of legislators has been calculated, the *IA*'s of all pairs can be aggregated, and the result can be divided by the total number of pairs. The resulting value is, of course, the mean agreement score of all pairs. As such, it represents a summary index of the group's cohesion. The mean could of course be supplemented by a measure of dispersion.

There are more complex and, for some purposes, more satisfactory ways of using index of agreement scores to measure intragroup cohesion. One other means is comparison of agreements among a group's members with agreements between these members and legislators outside the group. David Truman used this type of measure in examining the cohesion of state delegations and standing committees within the U.S. House of Representatives.[19] Truman lists for each member of the group being examined (a state delegation or a committee) the legislators with whom he had the highest scores. (The size of the group determines the number of scores listed. Truman listed scores equal to the number in the group minus one).

> Representative Wier's three highest agreements on the roll calls of the intermediate-cohesion set were with Representatives McCarthy of Minnesota, Blatnik of Minnesota, and Jacobs of Indiana. He thus had two intradelegation scores among his top three. The same procedure was followed for the three other men in the delegation, and the number of these intrastate scores in the delegation was then totaled. . . .
> If a delegation were perfectly cohesive, 'absences' excluded, the number of intrastate scores in this summation would be equal to the number of men in the delegation multiplied by one less than that number. That is, in the four-man Minnesota Democratic delegation the highest scores of each man

would be with his three state colleagues, giving a possible total of 12. The ratio of the actual number of scores to this theoretically possible number is an indicator of the frequency of intrastate agreements, a rough measure of the group's cohesion, and a basis of comparison with other delegations in the party.[20]

Some scholars have proposed measuring interpersonal agreement in somewhat more complex ways than we have described. One student of legislative voting has used phi-coefficients as measures of association on agreement between pairs. He aggregates these coefficients into a measure of group cohesion, which he terms an index of colligation.[21] Although the measures we have discussed may be imperfect, it is not clear to us that phi or any other statistic based on fourfold distributions offers a more adequate measure of interpersonal agreement than they do.[22]

A COMPARISON OF THE TWO TYPES OF COHESION MEASURE

A major difference between the Rice index and the indexes based on interpersonal agreements lies in the primary units that each analyzes. For the Rice index (or the indexes of absolute and relative cohesion), the individual roll call is taken into account and is analyzed as a unit. Average indexes of cohesion are calculated from Rice measures for a series of votes. In measures of cohesion based on interpersonal agreement, the unit of analysis is the *dyad*, or pair of legislators. A large number of roll calls must be taken into account to produce an accurate measure of agreement for one dyad, and a myriad of possible dyads must be analyzed. In other words, the Rice index measures cohesion first and foremost as a function of *aggregate group* action on single roll calls. The techniques for determining agreement of pairs focus primarily on cohesion as a function of *interpersonal, dyadic relationships.*

SOME MEASURES OF INTER-GROUP DIFFERENCE

The second characteristic of categoric groups frequently examined in roll-call studies is the difference between two or more groups in their response to a roll call or a set of roll calls.

The Index of Likeness.   The index of likeness is perhaps the simplest and most widely used measure of inter-group difference.[23] This index measures the difference between two groups in their response to a roll call. Simply defined, the index of likeness is the complement of the difference between the respective percentages voting "yea" in two groups. It is obtained by calculating the percentage of members of each group that voted in favor of the measure, subtracting the smaller percentage from the larger, and subtracting the remainder that operation produces from 100. The index varies from zero to 100; the former represents complete dissimilarity and the latter, complete similarity in group voting response.

The logic of the method is relatively straightforward. If 100 per cent of each party votes in support of the bill, the group response of each party is identical. This is also the case when the parties each split 80 per cent—20 per cent or 60 per cent—40 per cent. In all cases, the percentage of group members voting in the affirmative in the respective parties would be precisely the same, and this similarity would be shown in an index of 100. Conversely, when 100 per cent of the members of one group favor the bill while 0 per cent of the other group support it, there is 100 per cent—0 per cent or 100 per cent difference between the groups. The per cent difference is subtracted from unity to give $100\% - 100\% = 0$ as the index of likeness. The following examples illustrate the index.

Roll Call 25

Democrats: Yeas, 14; Nays, 50
Republicans: Yeas, 20; Nays, 13
  Per cent Democrats in affirmative $= 14/64 \times 100 = 22$
  Per cent Republicans in affirmative $= 20/33 \times 100 = 61$
  Index of Likeness $= 100 - (16 - 22) = 61$

Roll Call 38

Democrats: Yeas, 46; Nays, 13
Republicans: Yeas, 20; Nays, 11
  Per cent Democrats in affirmative $= 46/59 \times 100 = 78$
  Per cent Republicans in affirmative $= 20/33 \times 100 = 65$
  Index of Likeness $= 100 - (78 - 65) = 87$

One of the chief virtues of the index of likeness is its ability to sum up the differences in group support for a bill in a single, easily calculable measure. Index scores for single roll calls can be summed over a series of votes, and a mean index can then be determined for the series.

Chi-Square. The statistic known as chi-square (X^2) has been used to assess the existence of differences between two groups.[24] As applied to groups, the test provides a means of determining whether the difference in the portion of the representative groups voting "yea" and "nay" is larger than that expected by chance.

The computation of X^2 is relatively simple. The distribution of votes on a roll call for two groups is displayed in Table III-2.

TABLE III-2

Vote

		Yea	Nay	
	A	a	b	$a+b$
Groups				
	B	c	d	$c+d$
		$a+c$	$b+d$	N

Next, the expected distribution of responses is calculated: that is, the distribution that would exist if no differences between the two groups occurred. The expected distribution is determined for each cell by multiplying the column total by the row total and dividing by N. Thus, the expected frequency for cell a $= \dfrac{(a+c)\,(a+b)}{N}$. When the expected frequency is obtained for each cell, the difference between the expected and observed (actual) frequency is determined for each cell. This difference is squared, and the resultant figure is then divided by the expected frequency. The resulting quantities in each cell are then summed. This is the value of chi-square. The formula can be simply expressed:[25]

$$X^2 = \Sigma \ \frac{(fo - fe)^2}{fe}$$

where fo is observed frequency, and
fe is expected frequency.

The larger the difference between the observed and expected frequencies is, the larger the value of the chi-square will be. If the expected and observed frequencies are the same, the value of the chi-square will be zero. By looking at the sampling distribution of chi-square (available in almost all standard textbooks on statistics), we can determine the value of chi-square expected by chance at different levels of significance. We compare this value at some special level of significance (e.g., .05) with the value of the obtained X^2. If the latter figure is smaller, we can conclude that no significant difference exists between the two groups; if it is larger, we can conclude that a significant difference between them does exist.

The examples in Table III-3 illustrate the X^2 test applied to roll-call data.

TABLE III-3
CHI-SQUARE TABLES FOR FOUR VOTES

1.
VOTE
PARTY

	Yea	Nay	
Dems.	48	11	59
Reps.	24	7	31
	72	18	90

$X^2 = .20$
$p = >.05$ (non-significant)

2.
VOTE
PARTY

	Yea	Nay	
Dems.	54	3	57
Reps.	22	6	28
	76	9	85

$X^2 = 5.18$
$p = .05$

3.

VOTE

PARTY

	Yea	Nay	
Dems.	41	18	59
Reps.	29	1	30
	70	19	89

$$X^2 = 8.75$$
$$p = .01$$

4.

VOTE

PARTY

	Yea	Nay	
Dems.	3	57	60
Reps.	29	4	33
	32	61	93

$$X^2 = 64.80$$
$$p = .001$$

Note that the first fourfold table does not yield a significant value of X^2. One would intuitively expect this result, because members of both parties are more or less equally divided in their responses to the issue. Both Democrats and Republicans split their votes on the roll call, but approximately equal proportions of each party voted in favor of the measure. In short, no significant difference between the two groups obtains.

In the second roll call, a statistically significant X^2 value appears. By consulting a table of X^2 values, we find that a value of 5.18 is significant at the .05 level—that is, there are five chances out of one hundred that the distribution could have occurred by chance. The inference here is that party and response are not independent of one another. The two groups do differ.

The third example also is statistically significant. The obtained chi-square value of 8.75 has a probability of .01—meaning that this distribution could have occurred only by chance once out of one hundred times. Inspection of the table indicates that the Republican party was relatively cohesive on this measure, while the Democrats were somewhat divided. The concentration of responses in the "Rep-Y" cell of the matrix accounts for the largest portion of the value obtained in this distribution.

The final roll call is the one most easily interpreted, since most Democrats at that point opposed and most Republicans favored the measure. The high X^2 of 64.8 could have occurred by chance only once out of one thousand times. Thus, the researcher is relatively certain in this case that party affiliation and roll-call response are *not* independent of one another.

An important aspect of the chi-square test to remember when analyzing roll-call votes is that the measure will enable one to decide if a significant difference between two groups exists, but that it will not enable one to specify the degree of difference: The chi-square test will thus allow one to decide whether response is related to party (or whatever the group is), but it will not measure the *strength* of the relationship.

To measure the degree of relationship between group and response (the extent of the difference between two groups), one must turn to a measure of association. There are two measures of association that seem particularly useful in assessing intergroup differences: the phi-coefficient and Yule's Q.

Phi-Coefficient. The phi-coefficient is derived from the chi-square formula, and it can be shown that $\phi = \sqrt{X^2/N}$, where N represents the size of the sample.[26] Where the X^2 value has already been computed in the course of analysis, this formula may be used to convert the obtained X^2 to the ϕ measure of association. If one does not wish to test independence, but only to obtain phi directly, the formula noted earlier may be used:

$$\phi = \frac{ad - bc}{\sqrt{(a+b)\,(c+d)\,(a+c)\,(b+d)}}$$

where it is applied to a four-fold table of the type:

	Yea	Nay
Group A	a	b
Group B	c	d

The coefficient obtained will vary between -1 and $+1$. A test of significance may be made by converting phi to the corresponding chi-square value by means of the formula $\phi = \sqrt{X^2/N}$. The chi-square value can then be evaluated in any appropriate table of significance levels.

In the following table, phi-coefficients have been calculated for the same roll calls as were used above in the discussion of chi-square. Both values are given along with the value of ϕ/ϕ max.

(See note 27 for a discussion of ϕ/ϕ max.)

Roll Call	X^2	ϕ	ϕ/ϕ max	p
1	.2	.05	.07	(non-significant)
2	5.18	.25	.50	.05
3	8.75	—.31	.43	.01
4	64.8	—.83	.85	.001

The negative phi-coefficients we obtained in cases 3 and 4 are not of particular importance when only one roll call is considered at a time, because in such a case the researcher will have the original distribution before him as he analyzes the roll call. He can easily determine which party tended to vote in which direction; thus, the direction of the sign is not crucial to the substantive interpretation of the coefficient. However, when series of roll calls are to be compared by means of the coefficient, the signs will help differentiate among cases in which the parties voted in opposite directions. If both parties had split their votes similarly but in opposite directions, the coefficients would be the same, but the signs would be reversed. The following two cases will demonstrate this point.

	Yea	Nay			Yea	Nay	
Dems.	3	57	60	Dems.	57	3	60
Reps.	29	4	33	Reps.	4	29	33
	32	61	93		61	32	93

$$\phi = -.83 \qquad\qquad\qquad \phi = .83$$

Yule's Q. Yule's Q also can be used as a measure of inter-group differences. It is applied in the same manner as ϕ.[28]

$$Q = \frac{ad - bc}{ad + bc}$$

applied to a 2×2 table as follows:

	Yea	Nay
Group A	a	b
Group B	c	d

Applying the formula to the four tables shown earlier, we obtain:

Vote	Q
1	.12
2	.66
3	—.85
4	—.99

It should be noted that ϕ provides a measure of two-way association, whereas Q provides a measure of one-way association.[29] This feature of Q is sometimes very useful. For example, the inter-group difference in which the researcher is interested is the difference between two groups as sources of opposition or support for a given policy. In this case, he wants a measure that will reveal differences between the two groups in terms of the portion of total support or opposition each group supplies. Q provides such a measure. Maximum value is obtained whenever all the "yeas" or "nays" on a roll call are cast by one of the groups, no matter how many "yea" or "nay" voters there are. This can be seen in the next illustration.

Vote 1

	Yea	Nay	
Group A	25		25
Group B		50	50
	25	50	75

$$Q = 1.0$$
$$\phi = 1.0 \quad \left(\frac{\phi}{\phi\text{max}} = 1.0\right)$$
$$IL = 0$$

Vote 2

	Yea	Nay	
Group A	25		25
Group B	25	25	50
	50	25	75

$$Q = 1.0$$
$$\phi = .50 \quad \left(\frac{\phi}{\phi\text{max}} = .50\right)$$
$$IL = 50$$

These tables illustrate also differences between Q, on the one hand, and ϕ and the index of likeness, on the other. Although the value of Q is the same in both tables, the values of ϕ and the index of likeness differ from one table to the next. Both measures show the groups on vote 2 to be more alike (less different) than are the groups on vote 1. Thus, if the kind of difference between groups that is of interest to the researcher is the variation between groups in the proportion of respective group members supporting or opposing a given policy, then the index of likeness, or perhaps ϕ, is obviously a better measure than Q. Again, we see that the researcher must specify as clearly as possible the nature of the variable to be measured before selecting a means of measuring it. An instrument that is well suited for illustrating one aspect of a voting structure may obscure other aspects.

On occasion, the researcher may find it desirable to measure inter-group differences by the degree of accuracy with which he can predict from one variable (group affiliation) to another variable ("yea" or "nay" response). In such a case, the lambda coefficient of predictive association becomes a useful tool.

Lambda Coefficient. We interpret the lambda coefficient to be "the proportion by which we reduce the probability of error predicting the value of A when we know the value of B."[30] When a strong degree of association exists between categories A and B, our ability to predict one from the other increases considerably if we know the value of one of the variables. Applied to legislative voting analysis, this means that, if group affiliation and response to a roll-call vote are closely associated, we are better able to predict responses if we know the individual legislator's group identification.[31] Alternatively, we can say that if substantial differences between groups occur, our ability to predict response is greater if we know the legislator's group allegiance.

Although we will not concern ourselves here with the derivation of the lambda coefficient,[32] it may be useful to outline the logic and interpretation of the measure as follows: If the variable A (roll-call response) is randomly distributed in a cross-classification table, we have a 50-50 chance of predicting the value of A—that is, the probability of error in prediction is .50. Clearly, there is little value in being able to predict accurately in only fifty per cent of cases. But, if B (group affiliation) and A are associated, we will find that our error in predicting A will be decreased when we know the value of B. The amount of this reduction in error is given by lambda. Thus, a lambda coefficient of .45 indicates that our error in prediction is reduced by forty-five per cent.

The lambda coefficient for predicting A (voting response) is calculated according to the formula:[33]

$$\lambda A = \frac{\sum_{k} \max_{j} f_{jk} - \max_{j} f_j}{N - \max_{j} f_j}$$

where

f_{jk} is the frequency obtained in cell $(A_j B_k)$,

$\max_{j} f_{jk}$ is the largest frequency in row B_k,

$\max_{j} f_j$ is the largest marginal frequency

among the columns A_j.

The next example will illustrate the computational procedures involved in obtaining lambda coefficients for the A (response) variable. Three separate tables will be examined in a test of the hypothesis that *party* is a better predictor of roll-call response than the *urban-rural* nature of the constituency or the *socio-economic status* (SES) of the constituency. Each table represents the same roll-call vote, but responses are recombined according to the different categoric groups that we are examining.

TABLE III-4

LAMBDA COEFFICIENTS FOR THREE GROUPS

a
VOTE

PARTY

	Yea	Nay	
Dems.	8	52	60
Reps.	28	3	31
	36	55	91

$$\lambda A = \frac{52 + 28 - 55}{91 - 55} = \frac{25}{36} = .70$$

b
VOTE

CONSTITUENCY

	Yea	Nay	
Urban	2	28	30
Rural	34	27	61
	36	55	91

$$\lambda A = \frac{28 + 34 - 55}{91 - 55} = \frac{7}{36} = .20$$

c
VOTE

SOCIO-ECONOMIC STATUS

	Yea	Nay	
High	11	13	24
Low	25	42	67
	36	55	91

$$\lambda A = \frac{13 + 42 - 55}{91 - 55} = \frac{0}{36} = 0.$$

From this hypothetical example, we would conclude that party was more closely associated with voting patterns than were either of the constituency variables (*urban-rural, SES*). To put the point another way, there is more difference between the parties than there is between groups of legislators classified by type of constituency. No test of significance is connected to the lambda coefficient, since the reduction in error is given directly by the obtained value.

USING DATA ON INDIVIDUALS TO COMPARE GROUPS

It goes without saying that data on the voting behavior of individual legislators such as that produced by indexes discussed in the last chapter can be aggregated to provide data on groups of legislators. For example, the researcher interested in effect of section on party loyalty could categorize legislators into sectional groups and then aggregate the party loyalty index scores of the individuals in each group. He might then compare sectional groups by comparing the mean index computed for each group.

NOTES

[1] Legislative voting studies focusing upon political parties and using one or more of the methods discussed in this chapter are numerous. Examples include Julius Turner, *Party and Constituency* (Baltimore: Johns Hopkins Press, 1951); William J. Keefe "Party Government and Lawmaking in Illinois General Assembly," *Northwestern University Law Review*, 47 (March-April, 1952), 52-63; William J. Keefe, "Parties, Partisanship, and Public Policy in the Pennsylvania Legislature," *American Political Science Review*, 48 (June, 1954), 450-64; Malcolm E. Jewell, "Party Voting in State Legislatures," *American Political Science Review*, 49 (September, 1955), 733-91.

[2] Studies focusing upon regional groupings include V. O. Key, *Southern Politics in State and National* (New York: Alfred A. Knopf, 1951).

[3] See David R. Derge, "Urban-Rural Conflict: The Case in Illinois," in John C. Wahlke and Heinz Eulau (eds.), *Legislative Behavior: A Reader in Theory and Research* (Glencoe, Ill.: The Free Press, 1959), pp. 218-27; and Murray C. Havens, *City Versus Farm* (University, Ala.: University of Alabama Press, 1957).

[4] Duncan MacRae, Jr., "The Relation Between Roll Call Votes and Constituencies," *American Political Science Review*, 46 (December,

1952), 1046-55; also in Wahlke and Eulau, *Legislative Behavior,* pp. 197-203.

5 See, for example, Thomas A. Flinn, "Party Responsibility in the States: Some Causal Factors," *American Political Science Review,* 58 (March, 1964), 60-71; Lewis A. Froman, Jr., *Congressmen and Their Constituencies* (Chicago: Rand McNally and Co., 1963), Ch. 9; and MacRae, *op. cit.*

6 John B. McConaughy, "Certain Personality Factors of State Legislators in South Carolina," *American Political Science Review,* 44 (December, 1950), 897-903; also in Wahlke and Eulau, *op. cit.,* pp. 313-16.

7 Many research studies are relevant here. Among them are David B. Truman, *The Congressional Party: A Case Study* (New York: John Wiley and Sons, Inc., 1959); and Samuel C. Patterson, *Toward a Theory of Legislative Behavior; The Wisconsin State Assemblymen as Actors in a Legislative System* (unpublished doctoral dissertation, University of Wisconsin, 1958).

8 See Stuart A. Rice, *Quantitative Methods in Politics* (New York: Alfred A. Knopf, 1928), p. 209; and Rice's article, "The Behavior of Legislative Groups," *Political Science Quarterly,* 40 (1925), 60-72; reprinted in Wahlke and Eulau, *op. cit.* pp. 372-77.

9 As an example, see Truman, *op. cit.,* especially pp. 48-60.

10The early presentation of the index of cohesion in the Rice article, "The Behavior of Legislative Groups," *loc. cit.,* indicates the possible diversity of group identification that a researcher may find useful.

11Derge, *op. cit.,* p. 219.

12See Key, *op. cit.;* Turner *op. cit.;* and Jewell, *op. cit.*

13In John C. Wahlke, Heinz Eulau, William Buchanan, and LeRoy Ferguson, *The Legislative System: Exploration in Legislative Behavior* (New York: John Wiley and Sons, Inc., 1962), the authors make extensive use of many of these variables. The Patterson dissertation (*op. cit.*) is an earlier attempt to apply many of the same concepts to a single legislature.

14See David B. Truman, *op. cit.,* pp. 97-133, 193-246; and Duncan MacRae, Jr., "Roll Call Votes and Leadership," *Public Opinion Quarterly,* 20 (Fall, 1956), 543-58.

15For a critical view of the use of cohesion measures, see also Wilder Crane, Jr., "A Caveat on Roll-Call Voting Studies of Party Voting," *Midwest Journal of Political Science,* 4 (August, 1960) 237-49.

16The first extensive use of this method appeared in Herman C. Beyle, *Identification and Analysis of Attribute-Cluster-Blocs* (Chicago: University of Chicago Press, 1931). A more recent application can be found in Truman, *op. cit.*

17Arend Lijphart, "The Analysis of Bloc Voting in the General Assembly," *American Political Science Review,* 57 (December, 1963), 902-17.

[18]*Ibid,* 909-10.

[19]Truman, *op. cit.,* 247-78; also David B. Truman, "The State Delegation and the Structure of Party Voting in the United States House of Representatives," *American Political Science Review,* 50 (December, 1956), 1023-45.

[20]Truman, *The Congressional Party,* p. 251.

[21]John G. Grumm, "Means of Measuring Conflict and Cohesion in the Legislature," *Southwestern Social Science Quarterly,* 44 (March, 1964), 377-88. See also John G. Grumm, "The Systematic Analysis of Blocs in the Study of Legislative Behavior," *Western Political Quarterly,* 18 (June, 1965), 350-62.

[22]Phi or another measure of association such as Yule's Q measures a different aspect or dimension of interpersonal agreement than does a percentage measure. This can be seen clearly in the illustration. Each table shows a distribution of votes for a given pair of legislators. In each case, the pairs agree the same number and per cent of the time (on 14 out of the 20 roll calls; or 70 per cent). The phi values of the distributions vary considerably, however. The kind or type of interpersonal agreement measured by the simple frequency count or percentage might be termed "absolute" agreement. The kind of agreement measured by phi might be termed "relative" agreement to indicate that what is being measured is the degree of association between the votes of two legislators relative to given marginals. There may be cases in which interpersonal agreement can be better measured as "relative" agreement in contrast to "absolute" agreement, but it is not clear what these cases are.

Distribution of Vote on Twenty Roll Calls
for Five Pairs of Legislators

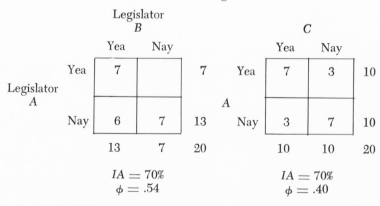

D

		Yea	Nay	
A	Yea	13		13
	Nay	6	1	7
		19	1	20

IA = 70%
$\phi = .31$

E

		Yea	Nay	
A	Yea	13	3	16
	Nay	3	1	4
		16	4	20

IA = 70%
$\phi = .06$

F

		Yea	Nay	
A	Yea	12	1	13
	Nay	5	2	7
		17	3	20

IA = 70%
$\phi = .28$

[23]The index was proposed by Stuart Rice in "The Behavior of Legislative Groups" (*op. cit.*). For an example of its use see Turner, *op. cit.*

[24]For a discussion of X^2, consult a standard statistics text. Discussions are found in William Hays, *Statistics for Psychologists* (New York: Holt, Rinehart and Winston, 1963); John Mueller and Karl Schuessler, *Statistical Reasoning in Sociology* (Boston: Houghton Mifflin Co., 1961); and Hubert Blalock, *Social Statistics* (New York: McGraw-Hill, 1960).

[25]A formula useful in computation of X^2 is:

$$X^2 = \frac{N\,(ad-bc)^2}{(a+b)\,(c+d)\,(a+c)\,(b+d)}$$

[26]For a discussion, see Mueller and Schuessler, *op. cit.*

[27]The phi coefficient is very sensitive to variations in marginal frequency. It is possible to obtain unity ($\phi = \pm 1$) only under particular conditions. These conditions are distributions with equal marginals. When marginals are unequal, the maximum obtainable value of phi is less than unity. In such cases, the obtained value of phi may underestimate the degree of association. The effect of un-

equal marginals can be corrected by expressing the coefficient as a ratio of the obtained value of phi to the maximum obtainable value of phi within the given marginals. The coefficient is described as phi over phi-max and is written $\dfrac{\phi}{\phi\text{max}}$. For a discussion of the problem and a formula for obtaining phi-max, see Mueller and Schuessler.

[28]For a discussion of Yule's Q, see *ibid.*

[29]*Ibid.*

[30]The following discussion is concerned primarily with lambda *a*, the statistic for predicting response from the group identification of the individual. Those familiar with lambda will recognize that we have presented only one of the set of lambda coefficients. The lambda *b* coefficient can also be calculated on the same data and will give the proportion of reduced error in prediction from variable *A*. In addition, there is a lambda *a-b* statistic that provides a symmetric measure of association taking into account the improvement in prediction in *both directions*. Since lambda *a-b* combines the properties of lambda-*a* and lambda-*b*, it will fall between those two values when all three are calculated on the same data. (The computer program CORR, described in the last chapter, calculates all three lambda values.)

In addition, it should be noted that lambda coefficients are not limited to dichotomous data as presented here. Polytomous variables (multiple response or group categories, for example) can be handled nicely by lambda. Further, lambda coefficients might be used to correlate one roll call with another, as well as to correlate group identification and voting response. For more information on the lambda statistic, the reader should consult the references below.

[31]An elaboration of the lambda formulation can be found in Hays, *op. cit.*, 606-10; and Leo A. Goodman and William H. Kruskal, "Measures of Association for Cross Classification," *Journal of the American Statistical Association,* 49 (December, 1954), 740-47.

[32]See *ibid.*

[33]Notation is taken from Hays, *op. cit.*

CHAPTER IV

THE IDENTIFICATION OF EMPIRICALLY DEFINED GROUPS: RICE-BEYLE CLUSTER-BLOC ANALYSIS

Chapter III described several methods of analysis used in measuring the internal cohesion of categoric or predetermined groups and in measuring differences between such groups. Categoric groups, as noted in Chapter I, are one of two types of group commonly examined in studies of roll-call voting. The second type was termed empirically defined groups, and we defined such groups as blocs or clusters of individuals who are discovered to have voted together regularly in a specified set of roll calls. Empirically defined groups, then, are clusters of legislators who have high levels of interpersonal agreement.

In order to analyze legislative voting in terms of empirically defined groups, the researcher must be able to identify in a population of legislators those legislators who regularly voted together. In this chapter we shall describe one major method of processing votes in such a way as to reveal clusters of interagreeing legislators. This method is called, after its inventors, Rice-Beyle cluster-bloc analysis.

Cluster-bloc analysis, like the indexes of cohesion and likeness discussed in Chapter III, was devised by Stuart Rice in the 1920's.[1] Herman Beyle developed and further elaborated the technique a few years later.[2] But, unlike the other techniques of roll-call analysis that Rice developed, cluster-bloc analysis has not been widely used by students of legislative voting despite its capacity to provide a great deal of information about the voting structure of legislative bodies. Undoubtedly, a major reason for the apparent neglect of cluster-bloc analysis is the computational difficulty it presents. The essential data in cluster-bloc analysis are indexes of agreement between pairs of legislators of the type discussed in Chapter III. The labor involved in computing these indexes limited the practical applicability of cluster-bloc analysis to research involving a very few roll calls, or to research on very small legislative bodies or groups. Today, the availability of computers makes possible cluster-bloc analysis in studies of the votes of large numbers of legislators on a large number of roll calls. The procedures involved in executing a cluster-bloc analysis and some uses of the technique will be described below.

PROCEDURES IN CLUSTER-BLOC ANALYSIS[3]

THE SELECTION OF ROLL CALLS FOR ANALYSIS

The first step in cluster-bloc analysis is the selection of roll calls to be analyzed, which will depend largely on the researcher's substantive or theoretical interests. The only limitation on selection imposed by the technique itself relates to the use of unanimous or nearly unanimous votes. Little or no purpose is served by subjecting a set of such votes to cluster-bloc analysis, for reasons that will soon be apparent. Apart from this restriction, the technique can be applied to any set of roll calls selected in terms of any criteria.

For the purposes of this discussion, let us assume that the researcher is interested in the bloc structure of a legislative party on issues that substantially divide that party. In this case, the criterion for selecting roll calls would be level of intra-party agreement. Using one of the indexes of cohesion discussed in Chapter III, the researcher would select roll calls falling within a specified range of cohesion. Suppose that there are one hundred roll calls in the legislative session that the researcher is studying. An examination of the cohesion displayed by the legislative party of interest to him shows that the party ranges in cohesion between an index of 0 and an index of 100 as measured by the Rice Index. The research calls for an examination of low cohesion votes. These the researcher defines as votes having an index of cohesion between 0 and 40. An examination of the one hundred roll calls reveals that fifty fall within this range. These fifty would constitute the sample of roll calls to be subjected to cluster-bloc analysis.

THE CALCULATION OF INDEXES OF AGREEMENT

Once the roll calls to be analyzed have been selected, the next step in executing cluster-bloc analysis is determination of the frequency with which every legislator agrees with every other legislator. It is now apparent why cluster-bloc analysis has not been used widely in voting studies. Except in the case of very small groups or of very small numbers of roll calls, the labor involved in calculating the frequency of agreement between every pair of legislators is enormous if the chore must be done without mechanical aids. Today, the availability of computers makes possible large-scale studies employing cluster-bloc analysis. Programs can readily be written for calculating the rate of agreement between all possible pairs of legislators. (See Chapter VIII for a discussion of one such program.)

To determine frequency of agreement, a researcher must first select a measure of agreement. In Chapter III, we described several alternative measures of agreement. A researcher can, of course, develop his own measure if none of these meets the needs of his research.

The most elementary measure of agreement is the number of times two legislators respond in the same way on a series of votes. Applying this measure in the example above, we would obtain a listing of all pairs of legislators and of the number of votes on which the members of the pair voted together. A computer will order the pairs in terms of frequency of agreement, normally listing first the pair with the highest rate (index) of agreement and then each subsequent pair in descending order. The outcome resembles the format of Table IV-1.

The first pair of legislators in Table IV-1, *A* and *B,* have an index of agreement of 47. This means that legislators *A* and *B* voted the same way on 47 of the 50 roll calls. The next pair, *A* and *C,* have the same index of agreement. The third pair, *A* and *D,* have an index of 46; they cast the same vote on 46 out of the 50 roll calls. In working with a legislative group of any size, the list

TABLE IV-1

Pair	Legislators	Number of Common Votes (Index of Agreement)
1	A and B	47
2	A and C	47
3	A and D	46
4	A and F	45
5	A and G	45
6	G and F	45
7	C and F	44
8	B and F	44
.	.	.
.	.	.
.	.	.
.	.	.
.	.	.

of agreement scores will be very long; the number of possible pairs in a legislative group is $\dfrac{N(N-1)}{2}$. If the researcher is interested only in pairs of legislators whose index of agreement lies above a specified level, he can reduce the length of the listed pairs by instructing the computer to record only pairs having agreement scores above the specified minimum.

As was noted in Chapter III, a simple frequency count as a measure of agreement of common votes is subject to certain criticisms. This measure has the effect of equating absences with disagreements. Two pairs of legislators have the following votes (zero indicates an absence):

$$A \quad O \ Y \ Y \ Y \ Y \ N \ N \ N \ N \ N$$
$$IA = 5$$
$$B \quad O \ N \ N \ N \ N \ N \ N \ N \ N \ N$$

$$A \quad O \ Y \ Y \ Y \ Y \ N \ N \ N \ N \ N$$
$$IA = 5$$
$$C \quad Y \ O \ O \ O \ O \ N \ N \ N \ N \ N$$

The index of agreement is the same for both pairs because (O-O) and (*N* or *Y*-O) combinations are treated in the same way as (*Y*-*N*) combinations.

There are at least two alternative ways of dealing with the problem of absences. As we mentioned in Chapter III, absences can be treated as missing data and excluded entirely from the computation of agreement scores. The following formula achieves this:

$$\text{Index of Agreement} = \frac{f}{t} \times 100$$

where *f* is the number of agreements, and
t is the total number of roll calls on which both legislators in a pair voted.

Applying this formula to the illustration above, we obtain:

Pair	IA
A and *B*	55
A and *C*	100

This provides a measure of agreement that is not affected by differences between pairs in the number of roll calls during which one or both members were absent.

The index developed by Arend Lijphart for use in the study of voting in the UN General Assembly has also been mentioned.[4] Lijphart wished to treat UN voting in such a way as to include abstentions in his calculations of agreements between nations. He argued that abstentions on a vote can be interpreted as a "partial agreement" with both sides. Accordingly, Lijphart proposed that the degree of agreement between pairs of nations be computed as follows:

$$\text{Index of Agreement} = \frac{f + \frac{1}{2}g}{t} \times 100$$

where *f* is the number of complete agreements between two nations,
g is the number of "partial" agreements (votes

on which one nation votes and the other abstains), and

t is the total number of votes cast by both nations in the pair.

Although this formula was developed to deal with abstentions and not with absences as such, for some purposes it might be desirable to treat absences in the same manner. Votes would be arranged in a 3×3 table:

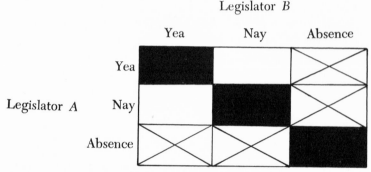

Legislator B

Votes falling in the three diagonal cells (including votes on which both members of the pair did not vote) could be treated as "complete" agreements. Votes falling in the four cells marked with an X could be treated as "partial" agreements. The index of agreement would be:

$$IA = f + \tfrac{1}{2}g$$

where f is the number of "complete" agreements, and
g is the number of "partial" agreements.

The effect of this measure of agreement contrasts sharply with that of the first measure described above. That measure has the effect of categorizing (O-O) and (Y-O or N-O) combinations in the same class as (Y-N) or (N-Y) combinations. In contrast, the measure just described has the effect of categorizing (O-O) combinations in the same class as (Y-Y) and (N-N) combinations and of placing (Y-O or N-O) combinations midway between agreement and disagreement. It would, of course, be possible to treat (O-O) combinations in the same way as (Y-O or N-O) combinations: that is, as cases of "partial" agreement. The formula would then be:

Index of agreement $= f + \frac{1}{2}g$

where f is the frequency of $(Y\text{-}Y)$ and $(N\text{-}N)$ combinations, and
g is the frequency of other combinations, i.e., $(Y\text{-}O$ or $N\text{-}O)$ and $(O\text{-}O)$.

All absences are placed midway between agreements and disagreements.

The researcher must decide which of these measures of agreement will best serve his needs. However, it should be noted that, if the researcher is interested in both agreement and disagreement, then the percentage of agreement index has a clear advantage over the other measures. Low indexes of agreement are equal, of course, to high indexes of disagreement; hence, the researcher can spot cases of high disagreement as well as cases of high agreement when this measure is used. This advantage is achieved, however, at the cost of treating absences as missing data and thus excluding them from the analysis. If the researcher finds it desirable to consider absences as a form of behavior rather than as missing data, he will want to use a measure that incorporates absences in the computation of agreement scores either by treating them as equivalent to disagreements, as does the first index we discussed, or by treating them as equivalent to agreements and/or behavior midway between agreement and disagreement, as do the two versions of the last index discussed.

THE PLACEMENT OF INDEXES OF AGREEMENT
SCORES IN A MATRIX

Once the researcher has calculated indexes of agreement between pairs of legislators, he must then in cluster-bloc analysis array these scores in matrix form. An example of a partial matrix is shown below. This is taken from David Truman's study of the voting structure of the legislative parties in the U. S. Senate during the 81st Congress.[5]

FIGURE IV-1

PORTIONS OF A MATRIX, SHOWING 23 DEMOCRATIC SENATORS WITH SCORES OF 59 OR HIGHER ON 74 SELECTED ROLL CALLS, 81ST CONGRESS, 2ND SESSION

	Neely, W. Va.	Kilgore, W. Va.	Humphrey, Minn.	Magnuson, Wash.	McMahon, Conn.	Lehman, N. Y.	Green, R. I.	Murray, Mont.	Anderson, N. M.	Myers, Pa.	Chavez, N. M.	Douglas, Ill.	Leahy, R. I.	Lucas, Ill.	Hill, Ala.	Sparkman, Ala.	McClellan, Ark.	Holland, Fla.	George, Ga.	Hoey, N. C.	Stennis, Miss.	Russell, Ga.	Chapman, Ky.
Neely, W. Va.	╲	68	65	63	62	61		60	58														
Kilgore, W. Va.	68	╲	64	60	59	58	58	59	61		60												
Humphrey, Minn.	65	64	╲	63	62	65	62	62		60		60	60										
Magnuson, Wash.	63	60	63	╲	60		59									Bloc							
McMahon, Conn.	62	59	62	60	╲	58		58		60				58									
Lehman, N. Y.	61	58	65		58	╲		58				58	59										
Green, R. I.		58	62	59			╲						59										
Murray, Mont.	60	59	62		58			╲															
Anderson, N. M.	58	61							╲														
Myers, Pa.			60		60					╲													
Chavez, N. M.		60									╲								Fringe				
Douglas, Ill.			60			58						╲											
Leahy, R. I.			60			59	59						╲					Bloc					
Lucas, Ill.					58									╲									
Hill, Ala.												Independent Nucleus			╲	63							
Sparkman, Ala.															63	╲							
McClellan, Ark.																	╲	67	60	60	63	58	59
Holland, Fla.																	67	╲	59	62	59		60
George, Ga.																	60	59	╲	63	59		
Hoey, N. C.																	60	62	63	╲			
Stennis, Miss.																	63	59	59		╲	63	61
Russell, Ga.																	58				63	╲	
Chapman, Ky.																	59	60			61		╲

Figure IV-1 demonstrates the primary purpose of arranging indexes of agreement scores in matrix form. Through arranging pairs in a matrix, we are able to discern blocs or clusters of inter-agreeing legislators. The matrix in the illustration shows pairs of legislators with agreement scores of at least 58. (Truman employed the simple index of agreement discussed above. These scores are simply the number of times two senators voted together on a set of 74 roll calls.) The matrix reveals two clusters or blocs. One, in the upper left-hand corner, consists of five senators mutually linked to one another by agreement scores of 59 or above. The other bloc, in the lower right-hand corner, consists of four senators with rates of agreement of at least 59. The matrix also provides other information. It shows what Truman terms "fringe" legislators: legislators having a minimal level of agreement with at least half the members of a bloc but not with all members.

The researcher must make two major decisions in organizing the matrix of agreement scores and in identifying blocs. One of these concerns defining blocs. A bloc can formally be defined as a cluster of pairs having agreement scores at or above a specified minimum. The researcher must specify what the minimum figure will be. This decision, like many other choices in roll-call analysis, is essentially substantive. It must be made in light of the researcher's purposes and in light of the assumptions he makes concerning the patterns he observes or seeks to observe in voting. The size and the structure of the blocs identified through cluster-bloc analysis will depend in part on the decisions made about minimum indexes of agreement. Generally, the higher the minimal level assigned is, the smaller in size and/or the fewer in number the blocs revealed by the matrix will be. Conversely, the lower the minimal level assigned is, the larger in size or number the blocs revealed by the matrix will be. We can see this by referring to the matrix shown earlier. The matrix includes no scores lower than 58; and blocs are defined as inter-agreeing pairs with scores of 59 or greater. Truman subsequently added to the matrix scores as low as 38. When progressively lower scores were added, the blocs grew in size. When scores down to 38 were added, the bloc shown in the upper left-hand corner, which consisted of five senators at the 59 level, grew to include eighteen members. In a similar way, the addition of scores increased the bloc in the lower right-hand corner from four members to fourteen.[6] (The matrix, of course, was larger than the one shown as new names were added with the decrease in scores.)

The researcher is likely to be interested in the bloc structure of a group at different levels of agreement. The matrix for this structure can be constructed by listing first only high agreement scores. The resulting structure can then be examined, and a record of it can be kept. Progressively lower scores can then be added. By keeping a record at each level, the researcher can reconstruct the bloc structure of the group at each of several levels of agreement.

In addition to selecting a minimal level of agreement by which to define blocs, the researcher must determine the way in which names are to be arrayed on the matrix. The formal criterion to be used here is simple. The pairs should be ordered so as to reveal upon completion of the matrix as complete a picture of the bloc structure of a group as is possible. This means that the matrix should reveal all possible blocs and also the most inclusive of all possible blocs. No one way of ordering pairs guarantees that this objective will be fully realized. Truman, after some experimentation, developed the procedures listed below as the ones most likely to reveal all possible blocs.[7] One of the authors of this book also has used these procedures and has found them satisfactory.

First, enter the highest agreement score in the appropriate cells in the upper left-hand corner of the matrix.

Second, search the list of pairs for the next highest agreement score between a pair that includes one of the members already listed on the matrix.

Third, continue in the same manner to search the list of pairs for legislators linked to one or more of the legislators already listed in the matrix. Note that the insertion of pairs is postponed until a pair occurs that includes one of the legislators already listed on the matrix. This requires a continual review of postponed pairs as each score is added to the matrix. The procedure, while laborious, appears to maximize the probability of producing a matrix that reveals a maximum number of blocs.

We have outlined the way in which matrixes can be constructed by hand. It is possible for this stage of the operation to be done by a computer. Computer construction may involve some information loss, as keeping a record of bloc structure at different levels of agreement may prove difficult, but the researcher may find that the time and energy saved is worth this cost.

SUMMARIZING THE INFORMATION OBTAINED
THROUGH BLOC ANALYSIS

Once the matrix is constructed and the blocs of inter-agreeing pairs are identified, information can economically be summarized for presentation. The Truman study provides an example of one form that such a summary can assume.[8] See Figure IV-2.

AN ILLUSTRATION OF THE USE OF
CLUSTER-BLOC ANALYSIS

As was indicated previously, Rice-Beyle cluster-bloc analysis has not been widely used in studies of legislative voting. Hence, little research exists that illustrates the uses to which the method can be put. David Truman's analysis of the congressional parties, to which we have often referred, is probably the most elaborate and extensive research making use of cluster-bloc analysis. Another example of its use is Arend Lijphart's study of voting alignments in the UN General Assembly.[9] Lijphart wished to identify and measure the cohesions of UN voting blocs on colonial issues. He selected a sample of 44 roll-call votes taken during the 1956, 1957, and 1958 sessions of the General Assembly. Lijphart describes how this sample was selected:

> The selection was made in the following manner: An adequate and generally acceptable definition of the term "colonial issues" proved extremely hard to find. Therefore, without attempting to define this politically loaded term, it was decided to regard the following questions as colonial issues during the 1956-1958 period: The Algerian, Cyprus, and West New Guinea questions, questions concerning trust territories and non-self-governing territories, and questions relating to the debate on the "right to self-determination." Of the many roll-call votes taken on these issues, 44 were selected as the "important" or "key" votes. Instead of sub-jectively choosing these, the following objective operational criterion was used: all non-unanimous votes on colonial issues were selected of which not only the numerical voting results but also the complete breakdown of the votes cast by each member state were reported in the 1956, 1957, and 1958 isues of the *Yearbook of the United Nations*. This meant, in

Figure IV-2

DEMOCRATIC CLEAVAGE: BLOC STRUCTURE OF SENATE DEMOCRATS ON 74 LOW-COHESION ROLL CALLS, 81ST CONGRESS, 2ND SESSION

Bloc I		Bloc II	
Members: 18		Members: 14	
Mean Score: 52.6		Mean Score: 50.7	
RANK		RANK	
1 Humphrey, Minn.			
2 Neely, W. Va. (s)			
3 Kilgore, W. Va.			
4 Magnuson, Wash.			
5 McMahon, Conn. (s)			
6 Lehman, N. Y.			
7 Green, R. I.			
8 Murray, Mont.			
9 Leahy, R. I.			
10 Anderson, N. M. (e)			X
11 Lucas, Ill. (e)			
12 Myers, Pa. (e)			
13 Douglas, Ill.			
14 O'Mahoney, Wyo. (s)			
15 Chavez, N. M. (s)			
16 Hill, Ala.			X
17 Benton, Conn.			
18 Taylor, Ida.			
		1 McClellan, Ark. (s)	
		2 Stennis, Miss.	
		3 Holland, Fla.	
		4 Hoey, N. C.	
		5 George, Ga. (s)	
		6 Chapman, Ky.	
	X	7 Russell, Ga.	
		8 Ellender, La.	
		9 Eastland, Miss.	
	X	10 Byrd, Va.	
		11 Connally, Tex. (s)	
	X	12 Robertson, Va.	
		13 McKellar, Tenn. (e)	
		14 Maybank, S. C. (s)	
FRINGE: 9		FRINGE: 3	
Sparkman, Ala.			X
Graham, N. C.			
McFarland, Ariz.			X
Hunt, Wyo.			
Pepper, Fla.			
Hayden, Ariz. (e)			X
Thomas, Utah (s)			X
O'Conor, Md.			
Kefauver, Tenn.			
		McCarran, Nev. (s)	
X		Johnson, Colo. (s)	
X		Johnston, S. C. (s)	

LEGEND: Each *bloc* member agreed with each other bloc member on 38 or more of the 74 votes in the set. *Mean score* of the bloc: the mean of the number of agreements between all pairs of bloc members. *Rank:* the rank of each bloc member according to the mean of his scores with all other bloc members, 1 designating the highest average number of agreements. *Fringe:* non-member having scores of 38 or higher with at least half of the bloc members. *X:* member of a bloc or fringe who had scores of 38 or higher with some but less than half the members of another bloc. (e): elective leader; (s): seniority leader.

fact, that the judgment of the UN Secretariat concerning the importance of the various roll-call votes was accepted.[10]

Lijphart next computed indexes of agreement for each pair of the UN's 79 nations, using as a measure of agreement the formula outlined in the last section, in which abstentions are treated as "partial" agreements. The indexes for each of the pairs of the 79 nations were then arranged in a 79 × 79 matrix. Lijphart first analyzed only very high indexes of agreement, and then progressively lower indexes, in order to discover the exact levels at which blocs appeared. He was able to summarize much of the resulting information about bloc structure in graphic form. Figure IV-3 shows the voting alignments that emerged at the 95.5 per cent level of agreement.[11]

The figure reveals the existence of several blocs of nations and the existence of other nations that were partially aligned with these blocs.

The bloc composed of the Soviet Union, its two Union Republics, and its East European satellites was 100 per cent solid with the exception of Poland. Another bloc at the 95.5 per cent level was the group of Iraq, Saudi Arabia, Jordan, and Libya, all belonging to the Arab Caucusing Group. A number of other, primarily Afro-Asian states were loosely connected with this group. Among the European and Commonwealth nations, there were three voting blocs at the 95.5 per cent level: the Danish-Norwegian-Swedish bloc, and two interconnected blocs composed of West European states and English-speaking nations of the British Commonwealth.[12]

Lijphart then included scores between 95.5 and 87.5. This revealed a considerably more complex voting structure, which is graphically portrayed in Figure IV-4.[13]

The Soviet bloc merged with a number of Afro-Asian nations to form a large bloc composed of 20 states. A smaller bloc, consisting of Ceylon, Ethiopia, Tunisia, Greece, and Yugoslavia also appeared at this level. These two blocs were closely interconnected. In fact, an overlapping voting bloc emerged, composed of six states of the large bloc and four states of the small bloc. In order not to confuse the general picture by drawing too many lines, the interconnections between these ten states are indicated by the shaded area in

FIGURE IV-3

VOTING ALIGNMENTS AT THE 95.5 PER CENT LEVEL

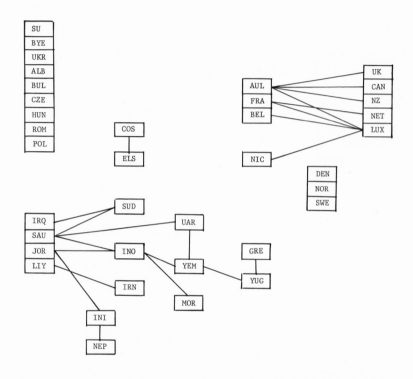

Code: States are identified by the first three letters of their official English names, e.g., BEL = Belgium, COS = Costa Rica, ELS = EL Salvador, except for the following abbreviations:

AUL —Australia   LIB —Liberia
AUS —Austria   LIY —Libya
CHE—Chile   NZ —New Zealand
CHA—China   SA —Union of South Africa
INI —India   SU —Soviet Union
INO —Indonesia   UAR—United Arab Republic
IRN —Iran   UK —United Kingdom
IRQ —Iraq   US —United States

FIGURE IV-4

VOTING ALIGNMENTS AT THE 87.5 PER CENT LEVEL

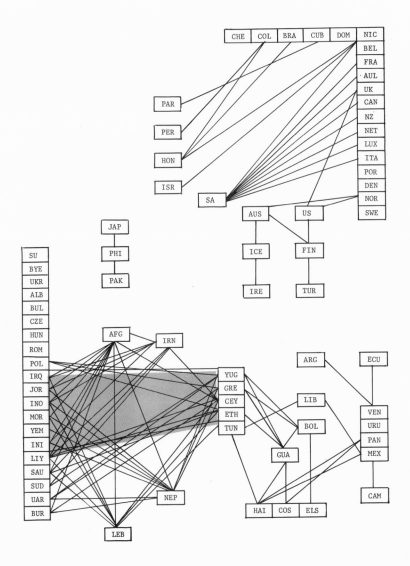

[the] figure. . . . Three blocs of Latin American states appeared at the 87.5 per cent level; the two smaller of these were relatively closely aligned. The largest Latin American voting bloc was more closely aligned to the European and Commonwealth group. Nicaragua, which is drawn between the two blocs, belonged to both voting blocs at the 87.5 per cent level. The Scandinavian, West European, and Commonwealth states which formed three blocs at the 95.5 per cent level, constituted a single bloc together with Italy and Portugal at the 87.5 per cent level.[14]

THE PROBLEM OF INFERENCE

Cluster-bloc analysis, like all other methods of roll-call analysis, provides a means by which voting behavior can be described and measured; but it cannot, by itself, provide the information necessary to an adequate explanation of the patterns that are revealed.

Agreement in voting can result from at least four distinguishable sources. First, even if all legislators voted independently of one another, it is very likely that some pairs of legislators would register higher agreement than other pairs. Second, agreement can result from legislators holding similar attitudes toward a set of issues. Third, agreement can result from group pressure and loyalty. Fourth, agreement in a series of roll calls may result from bargaining arrangements between individuals or between groups of which the individuals are members. From the existence of blocs, the researcher may attempt to infer that one or more of these factors is operating to produce the observed blocs; but the researcher should be fully aware of what he is doing. The voting data can be suggestive and even supportive of inferences about the causes of the legislators' behavior, but such data alone cannot validate the researcher's inferences. The researcher must look to information about legislators beyond data on their voting to test his inferences about the factors that explain the emergence of certain voting blocs or, for that matter, any other pattern in voting.[15]

NOTES

[1] Stuart A. Rice, "The Identification of Blocs in Small Political Bodies," *American Political Science Review,* 21 (August, 1927), 619-27; reprinted in Stuart A. Rice, *Quantitative Methods in Politics* (New York: Alfred A. Knopf, 1928), Chapter 16.

[2] Herman C. Beyle, *Identification and Analysis of Attribute-Cluster-Blocs* (Chicago: University of Chicago Press, 1931).

[3] This description of procedure is based in large part upon David Truman's discussion. See David Truman, *The Congressional Party* (New York: John Wiley and Sons, Inc., 1959), particularly pp. 45-48 and 320-26.

[4] Arend Lijphart, "The Analysis of Bloc Voting in the General Assembly: A Critique and a Proposal," *American Political Science Review,* 57 (December, 1963), 902-17.

[5] Truman, *op. cit,* p. 46.

[6] Truman, pp. 46-48.

[7] Truman, p. 325.

[8] Truman, p. 55.

[9] Lijphart, *op. cit.*

[10] Lijphart, p. 911.

[11] Lijphart, p. 914.

[12] Lijphart, p. 913.

[13] Lijphart, p. 915.

[14] Lijphart, p. 913.

[15] For a discussion of the problem of inference in the context of David Truman's analysis, see Austin Ranney's "Review of *The Congressional Party,*" *American Political Science Review,* 54 (March, 1960), 220-21.

As noted in the first chapter, several of the techniques used in studies of legislative voting have been used also in studies of judicial voting. For illustrations of the use of bloc analysis in judicial studies, see C. Herman Pritchett, *The Roosevelt Court: A Study of Judicial Politics and Values, 1937-1947* (New York: Macmillan, 1948); Glendon Schubert, *Quantitative Analysis of Judicial Behavior* (Glencoe, Ill.: The Free Press, 1959), Ch. 3; and Eloise C. Snyder, "The Supreme Court as a Small Group," *Social Forces,* 36 (March, 1958), 232-38.

CHAPTER V SOME METHODS OF SELECTING
ROLL CALLS FOR ANALYSIS

Roll-call studies can be grouped into two categories: studies based on analysis of single roll calls; and studies based on analysis of a number of roll calls.

STUDIES OF SINGLE ROLL CALLS

Occasionally, students of legislative voting examine only one roll call. As Duncan MacRae observes:

> This procedure is not without value, for the detailed study of a single roll call can give insight into the legislative process. It is particularly valuable when the single roll call deals with some significant variable, so that the findings can be generalized.[1]

Most studies of legislative voting, however, involve the examination of more than one vote.

STUDIES OF AGGREGATIONS OF ROLL CALLS

We can divide studies of legislative voting based on examination of several roll calls into two types: studies based on the analysis of the total population of roll-call votes; and studies based on samples of roll-call votes. In the first case, the researcher examines all roll-call votes taken in a legislative body during the time period of interest to him. This type of study is rare. Most roll-call studies entail the analysis of one or more samples of roll-call votes rather than the analysis of total populations. Thus, the selection of roll calls to be included in the set of votes to be analyzed is a crucial element in most roll-call research. We have mentioned the problem of selection in previous chapters, and we shall now look at the matter more systematically.

POLICY-RELATED SELECTION CRITERIA

Some types of roll-call research, as we have noted, call for analysis of votes on issues relating to a particular area of public policy, e.g., social welfare, foreign relations, public works, and the like. The researcher's task is to select from a population of roll calls those that relate to the policy or issue area (or areas) being studied. In discussing indexes in Chapter II, we noted the kinds of problems the researcher encounters in using policy-oriented criteria to select roll calls. We noted that his subjective judgment can be in error. He may include within his sample roll calls that do not in fact belong to the sample, or he may exclude roll calls that should be included in the sample. It was noted that Guttman scaling provides one means of partially overcoming this problem. In Chapter VI, we shall discuss how Guttman scaling procedures can be used as either a supplement to or a substitute for subjective judgment in selecting roll calls relating to given dimensions of public policy or issue controversy.

SYSTEMATIC, NON-POLICY-RELATED CRITERIA OF SELECTION

If the researcher does not desire to limit his research to a particular area of public policy, or if it is desirable to analyze a *representative* sample of roll calls, the topical selection criteria will not be useful in making the necessary limiting choices. It will be necessary to employ some "objective" criteria in the selection process in order to reduce the mass of roll-call data to manageable size. Two common techniques for this type of selection are *systematic sampling* and *random sampling*.

If the total number of recorded roll calls in a particular session is 900 and the researcher wants no more than 100 in his study, a simple way to reduce the number is to choose systematically every ninth roll call. This, however, has serious difficulties, because the most important bills might be clustered together near the end of the legislative session. If so, this kind of systematic sampling would underestimate the important bills and over-represent the less important bills considered at the beginning of the session.

A better solution is to enumerate each bill and select from the list using a set of random numbers. This method should eliminate the temporal bias and remove whatever subjective selection criteria the researcher might unconsciously impose on his data. Randomizing has the same effect as selecting roll calls out of a hat, but it can be accomplished more simply by referring to a table of random numbers. Such tables are available in most standard statistics handbooks.[2]

However desirable randomizing may seem to the researcher who wants to be as "scientific" as possible, there are many circumstances in which it is neither practical nor theoretically justifiable to use random selection. The most common situation of this type occurs when the researcher wishes to study only those roll calls that were strongly contested in the legislature. In such a case, the selection procedure will probably be based on one or both of the following criteria: (1) the number of members voting on the issue at the roll-call stage (degree of participation); (2) the number of members voting against the majority stand on the issue (degree of contesting).

The first criterion may be used to eliminate all roll calls in which a certain minimum number of legislators does not participate. The minimum may be specified arbitrarily by the researcher prior to the selection process, and he is at liberty to make the requirement as stringent as he chooses. The only practical considerations that enter into the choice of a proper minimum is the rate of absenteeism prevalent in the legislature. In some legislatures, for example, an arbitrary minimum of 75 per cent (present and voting) would eliminate all but a handful of roll calls, and the risk of deleting important roll calls would be considerable. On the other hand, a legislature in which absenteeism is very low would enable one to specify a higher minimum as the cut-off point.

The degree of contesting is also a useful criterion for selection, because in many legislatures the number of unanimous roll-call votes is often large. For most studies, a unanimous vote indicates little about the conflicts and cleavages present in the legislature. As a result, a large amount of energy would be wasted in considering unanimous votes. (William Keefe found that 1,049 out of 1,285 roll calls in the 1951 Pennsylvania Senate were uncontested; only the remaining handful demonstrated any evidence of conflict or factionalism in the legislature.)[3]

The choice of an appropriate cut-off point for gauging the degree of contesting is again arbitrary, and it may vary with the needs of the individual investigator. A simple way to eliminate unanimous roll calls is to record only those on which at least one legislator opposed the majority position. One may also choose to be more stringent by accepting only those roll calls on which at least 10 per cent of the membership dissents. The eventual choice will depend on the amount of conflict that the investigator wants to incorporate in his analysis.[4]

It is possible to combine both criteria (participation and contesting) into a composite, two-stage selection process. To do this, one need only record the marginal totals of the roll calls (number of members voting "yea" and "nay") and specify the minimum participation and minimum opposition that are acceptable to him. Each roll call can be checked first against one criterion, then against the other, to determine whether it meets minimum conditions for inclusion in the analysis. The result may be a sample of roll calls on which, say, 75 per cent of the members were voting and more than 10 per cent opposed the majority.

Another possible procedure for selecting roll calls was used by David Truman in *The Congressional Party*. Professor Truman calculated a Rice index of cohesion for each roll call in his sample and used the resulting cohesion values to divide the sample into three groups—having "high," "medium," and "low" cohesion.[5] His purpose was to examine the behavior of voting coalitions under varying conditions of party cohesion. The Rice technique made it possible to differentiate among roll calls on the basis of party cohesion. There is no apparent reason why this procedure could not be used in any case in which it is desirable to hold cohesion constant while studying some other aspect of voting.

EMPIRICAL COMBINATION OF SELECTION CRITERIA—
THE COEFFICIENT OF SIGNIFICANCE

The two-step method of roll-call selection, in which one sequentially applies criteria of (1) participation and (2) contesting, bears with it an inherent methodological and theoretical difficulty. If two principles are to be used in selecting the sample, how much weight is to be given each of the criteria? Certainly, each gives different results; and the final sample of roll calls selected will reflect the way in which the criteria are juggled. For example, one would have a different set of roll calls using values of 75 per cent and 10 per cent participation and contesting than if he used 80 per cent and 5 per cent. Professor William H. Riker has proposed an empirical method for combining both criteria into a single value, thereby avoiding the ambiguity of the two-stage method.

The proposed alternative involves the use of a "significance value," which represents a numerical index mathematically derived from (1) the number of members present and voting on a particular measure, and (2) the degree to which the outcome of the issue is contested. "Significance," defined in this manner, is actually a composite index of "participation" and "conflict." The most significant roll call is one in which all members of the legislature are present and voting and in which there is the maximum possible division of responses (maximum participation, maximum conflict). The least significant roll call is one in which only a quorum is present and all vote together (minimum participation, minimum conflict).

The illustration that follows has been adapted from Riker's original presentation to demonstrate this theory of "significance."[6]

In the matrix of outcomes, the upper left-hand corner shows the "most significant" roll-call votes; the lower right area of the matrix contains the "least significant" outcomes. The value that each roll call receives is a function of its position in the matrix, and it can be derived by adding the row and column positions of the particular outcome. For example, the significance value of outcome 5-4 is $1 + 1 = 2$; for outcome 6-1, it is $3 + 3 = 6$; for

FIGURE V-1

EXAMPLE OF THE MATRIX OF OUTCOMES IN A SIMPLE LEGISLATURE

Row Number		Column Number			
	1	2	3	4	5
1	5-4	6-3	7-2	8-1	9-0
2	5-3	6-2	7-1	8-0	
3	4-3	5-2	6-1	7-0	
4	4-2	5-1	6-0		
5	3-2	4-1	5-0		

n = number of members = 9
t = a quorum = 5
r_i = number voting on a roll call
m = minimum necessary for victory = $\dfrac{r_i}{2} + 1$

out come 5-0, it is $5 + 3 = 8$. By definition, the significance value will have a minimum of 2, and that value will be assigned to those roll calls on which all members are present and a maximum division of the vote occurs. The least significant value in the matrix will fall in the lower right-hand section of the diagram; its numerical magnitude will depend on the size of the legislature. In this example, the values vary from 2 (most significant) to 8 (least significant).

The average researcher will not find it desirable or perhaps even possible to construct a similar matrix of outcomes for his legislature, especially if it has a membership of several hundred. But since each possible outcome has been defined mathematically in terms of the notation scheme given above, it is possible to express a general procedure for obtaining the significance value without constructing a matrix. The following formula will give the same significance value that would be obtained by adding row and column totals in the matrix:[7]

$$v(a_{ij}) = n - q_{ij} - m + 2 + \frac{n - r_i + 1}{n - t + 2}$$

where a_{ij} is any possible outcome,

$v(a_{ij})$ is the value of a_{ij},

n is the number of members of the legislature,

r_i is the number voting on a roll call in which the outcome is a_{ij},

q_{ij} is the number on the losing side of a_{ij},

m is the minimum necessary for victory when r_i participate, and

t is a quorum.

The higher the numerical value obtained from this formula is, the lower the "significance" of the roll call will be. The investigator can easily rank-order his sample of roll calls on the basis of the obtained significance values and select votes from the range of values most relevant to the study.

It has already been noted that the values that the outcomes can obtain depend on the size of the legislature; thus, the least significant outcome of the U.S. House of Representatives will differ considerably from that of the Senate (*ca.* 328 as opposed to *ca.* 77). To remedy this situation and to make the measure comparable from one legislature to another, Riker introduces the "significance coefficient," which is described in the formula

$$s = 1 - \frac{v(a_{ij}) - v(a_{11})}{v(a_{dg}) - v(a_{11})}$$

where $v(a_{ij})$ is the value of outcome a_{ij},

$v(a_{dg})$ is the value of the least significant outcome, and

$v(a_{11})$ is the value of the most significant outcome.[8]

The value of s falls between 0 and 1. It can be seen that s will be zero only when $v(a_{ij}) = v(a_{dg})$: that is, when it is the least significant outcome. Conversely, s can only attain the value of one when $v(a_{ij}) = v(a_{11})$: that is, when it is the most significant outcome. This formula conforms more closely to a familiar sense of order, because a high index value represents high "significance" and *vice versa*.

The following example will illustrate the computational procedures involved in obtaining a significance coefficient for a hypothetical roll-call vote in a one-hundred-man legislature:

Roll Call a_{ij}: Yeas, 45; Nays, 52

n = number of members in the legislature = 100

r_i = number voting on the issue = 45 + 52 = 97

q_{ij} = number on the losing side = 45
m = minimum necessary for victory when r (97) participate
= 49
t = quorum = 51

Substituting in the formula for obtaining the significance value, we get:

$$v(a_{ij}) = 100 - 45 - 49 + 2 + \frac{100 - 97 + 1}{100 - 51 + 2} = 8 + \frac{4}{51} = 8.08$$

To convert $v(a_{ij})$ to a significance coefficient, we must first find the values for $v(a_{11})$ and $v(a_{dg})$. The distribution of votes on the roll calls of maximum and minimum significance would be:

$v(a_{11})$ — 51-49
$v(a_{dg})$ — 51-0

Substituting in the appropriate formula, we get:

$$v(a_{11}) = 100 - 49 - 51 + 2 + \frac{100 - 100 + 1}{100 - 51 + 2} = 2 + \frac{1}{51} = 2.02$$

$$v(a_{dg}) = 100 - 0 - 26 + 2 + \frac{100 - 51 + 1}{100 - 51 + 2} = 76 + \frac{50}{51} = 76.98$$

To obtain the significance coefficient, we substitute the appropriate values and obtain:

$$s = 1 - \frac{8.07 - 2.02}{76.98 - 2.02} = 1 - \frac{6.06}{74.96} = 1 - .08 = .92$$

In this example, none of the mathematical calculations was carried out beyond the second decimal place. In most cases, this is probably sufficient to distinguish among the various roll calls in a given set. If added discrimination is desired, it is possible to carry out the calculations to the fourth decimal, as Riker suggests. Doing so will virtually insure that a unique numerical value for each roll call outcome will be obtained, so that the entire set can be rank-ordered conveniently.

APPLICATION OF THE SIGNIFICANCE COEFFICIENT

The procedure for obtaining significance values and significance coefficients was originally presented as an alternative to the two-step application of selection criteria. Rather than eliminating sequentially roll calls that fall below a minimum participation and conflict level, we can now calculate a value that incorporates both criteria. The entire set of roll calls can be ordered in terms of this single range of values, and the investigator can choose those roll calls that satisfy the requirements of his research design.

The use of the significance coefficient as a means of ordering and selecting roll calls for further analysis, however, is only one possible application of the technique. Any measure that orders a set of data on a meaningful dimension is inherently useful in a variety of ways. For example, if we can assume that the significance coefficient does in fact measure the amount of conflict manifested at the roll-call voting stage,[9] it would be possible to test hypotheses about issue conflict in the legislature. Space in a book of this type is insufficient to elaborate these notions fully, but the suggestions that follow may prove useful.

It is commonplace to note that the importance of various issues changes in the passage of time. Although civil rights may be important in current legislative activity, they may not invoke much emotion a century from now. Debate over protectionist tariffs, entry into international organizations, farm-price supports, and the expansion of government activities are all policy matters that vary in impact from one legislative session to another. In other words, their *salience* for the legislature may vary considerably. It seems possible that *issue salience* could legitimately be measured using the coefficient of significance.

The procedure for such an operation would probably be to divide roll calls into categories of varying policy concern. Significance coefficients could be calculated for each set, and the average significance value for each *set* could be calculated. It would be feasible to use these average coefficients to compare the salience of one policy area with that of another. This could be done within one session of the legislature, in order to discover which set of bills generated the most heat during that period.

Comparisons might also be made from one session to another. One could calculate average coefficients of significance for the same policy area (say, regulation of business) in a number of different legislative sessions. This would permit construction of a longitudinal trace line of issue significance as the salience of an issue changed during a historical period.

An extension of this logic suggests that it would be possible also to test the salience of a particular policy area in legislatures of different political units; for example, in various state legislatures. Variations in issue salience from one state to another (or even from one country to another) might provide an interesting clue to the political culture of the units compared.

Although its lack of use to date encourages caution, it appears that the Riker method for determining significance coefficients has sufficient potential as an ordering and hypothesis-testing device to warrant further use by students of legislative behavior. One of the major drawbacks of the significance coefficient is the rather tedious mathematical calculation it involves. Understandably, few researchers have been willing to invest the time and energy necessary to obtain the significance coefficients of a large number of roll calls. However, part of this difficulty can be alleviated by electronic data processing, which can take the tedium out of the manipulations. There is currently at least one computer routine available that can perform the task relatively inexpensively and easily. Readers interested in such a program should consult Chapter VIII.

NOTES

[1] Duncan MacRae, *Dimensions of Congressional Voting* (Berkeley: University of California Press, 1958), p. 301. For an example of the type of research that can be done on one roll-call vote, see Milton C. Cummings, Jr., and Robert L. Peabody, "The Decision to Enlarge the Committee on Rules: An Analysis of the 1961 Vote," in Robert L. Peabody and Nelson W. Polsby (eds.), *New Perspectives on the House of Representatives* (Chicago: Rand McNally and Company, 1963).

[2] See, for example, Herbert Arkin and Raymond R. Colton, *Tables for Statisticians* (New York: Barnes & Noble, Inc., 1963).

3 William J. Keefe, "Parties, Partisanship, and Public Policy in the Pennsylvania Legislature," *America Political Science Review*, 48 (June, 1954), 451.

4 Remember that "conflict" is a property inferred from the amount of opposition at the voting stage. Such a quantitative measure does not include such relevant criteria as the mood of the legislators, the amount of anger generated before and after the vote was taken, and the like. These admittedly useful data must be supplied from qualitative information available from newspaper accounts, interviews, and the like.

5 David B. Truman, *The Congressional Party: A Case Study* (New York: John Wiley and Sons, Inc., 1959), pp. 48-50.

6 William H. Riker, "A Method for Determining the Significance of Roll Calls in Voting Bodies," in John C. Wahlke and Heinz Eulau (eds.), *Legislative Behavior: A Reader in Theory and Research* (Glencoe, Ill.: The Free Press, 1959), pp. 379-80. The presentation follows closely parts of Professor Riker's discussion.

7 Since it is possible for roll calls with different row and column positions to have the same outcome in terms of the significance values, the correction factor

$$\frac{n - r_i + 1}{n - t + 2}$$

is added to prevent roll calls with different marginal totals from having the same value. Formulas and notation are taken from Riker, *op. cit.*, p. 379

8 Riker, p. 380.

9 For a discussion of the assumptions of the method and of possible objections to it, see Riker, especially pp. 380-83.

CHAPTER VI

METHODS FOR SELECTING ROLL CALLS, DESCRIBING THE BEHAVIOR OF INDIVIDUAL LEGISLATORS, AND IDENTIFYING GROUPS OF LEGISLATORS: GUTTMAN SCALE ANALYSIS

In Chapter I, we observed that methods of roll-call analysis serve three purposes: the characterization of roll calls; the characterization of the voting behavior of individual legislators; and the characterization of the voting behavior of groups of legislators. All the techniques that we have described up to this point serve one or two of these purposes, but none of them satisfies all three. In this chapter and in the next, we shall discuss two methods of roll-call analysis that do serve all three purposes— that can be used in selecting roll calls for analysis, in characterizing and measuring the behavior of individual legislators, in identifying empirically defined groups of legislators, and in analyzing categoric groups. The first of these two methods, the one described in this chapter, is Guttman scale analysis.

THE GENERAL PURPOSE OF SCALE ANALYSIS

Scale analysis was initially developed by Louis Guttman as a means of determining whether a series of attitude questions on interview schedules measured a common underlying attitude.[1] For example, a researcher is interested in ethnocentricity. He assumes individuals in a population differ in the degree of their ethnocentricity. The researcher devises a set of items, the response to which he believes will measure these variations. The question now comes up: Do all of the items relate to ethno-centricity, or are they tapping a variety of different attitudes? By adding together an individual's responses to a series of items, is one in fact adding similar elements, or are apples being added to oranges, perhaps, along with plums? If the individual items do relate to diverse attitudes rather than to a single attitude—eth-nocentricity—then the set of items obviously does not provide a valid measure of variations in ethnocentricity. Guttman developed his scaling procedures to deal with this type of problem.

In Chaper II, discussing the construction of indexes, we ob-served that the same type of problem exists in roll-call analysis. The researcher is interested in measuring variation among legis-lators in their support of social welfare programs. He examines a population of roll calls and selects as a measuring instrument a set of roll calls. His problem is essentially the same as that confronting the researcher who seeks to use questionnaire items as a measure of ethnocentricity. Is his measuring instrument uni-dimensional? Do the roll calls he has selected belong together in that each relates to one common, underlying dimension? For example, the researcher might select ten roll calls that he be-lieves relate to "social welfare" and, hence, provide a means by which to measure variation in the support given "social welfare" programs among a group of legislators. It is possible that of these ten votes the legislators respond to only six as "social welfare" issues. On the remaining four, their voting relates to some other variable, e.g., support of the executive's program or support of political party. On the other hand, the researcher may be correct in assuming that the ten roll calls do involve a response to a common variable. The important point is that the researcher cannot know simply from examining the content of roll calls whether his assumption about commonality is correct. His as-sumption should be empirically tested, and Guttman scaling provides one means of doing so.

Guttman scaling involves an examination of the patterns that are formed by legislators' responses to a set of roll calls.[2] If the voting behavior of legislators is indeed capable of description according to a single dimension or variable, e.g., supporting social welfare programs, this fact will be revealed by the pattern or configuration formed by the votes on the roll calls.

This point can best be made if we use as an illustration a variable less complex than *attitude toward social welfare*. A conventional example is *height*. Imagine that a legislative body votes on the following questions:

1. Are you five feet tall or more?
2. Are you five feet, six inches or more?
3. Are you six feet or more?

How would we expect the pattern of responses to these questions to look? We would expect the votes of all legislators to fall into one of the four patterns in Table VI-1.

TABLE VI-1

Question 1	Question 2	Question 3
Yes	Yes	Yes
Yes	Yes	No
Yes	No	No
No	No	No

We would expect to observe this pattern of votes because all three questions clearly relate to a single variable—height. We would therefore expect all members who were six feet or over to answer "yes" to all three questions. Those who were five feet, six inches or more, but less than six feet (those who possess the variable to a lesser degree) would be expected to answer "yes" to questions one and two, but "no" to question three. Those who possessed the variable to an even lesser degree (those between five feet and five feet, six) would be expected to answer "yes" to question one, but "no" to questions two and three. Finally, those who possessed the minimum of the variable (were under five feet) would be expected to answer "no" to all three questions.

We can present this notion graphically by showing the continuum or dimension (in the illustration, height) as a straight line. The line can then be divided into segments and lettered. Each segment represents a position on the continuum. Individuals are located in one of these segments by the degree to which they possess the variable.

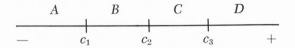

The continuum runs from left to right, with those possessing the least of the variable falling on the extreme left (the shortest individuals) and those possessing the most of the variable (the tallest individuals) falling on the extreme right.

Choices can be conceived of as cutting this continuum at different points, as is shown in the figure by $c_1 \ldots c_3$. The "easiest question" (c_1) cuts the continuum furthest to the left, and the "hardest question" cuts it furthest to the right. "Ease" and "hardness" can be non-operationally considered as the degree to which an individual must possess the variable in order to respond positively to the issue. For example, in our three questions, question three (Are you six feet or over?) is the hardest, because only those who possess the most of the variable (only the tallest individuals) will respond positively to it. In operational terms, "ease" and "hardness" of issues are defined by the frequency of positive responses. An issue on which 90 per cent of the respondents respond positively is an "easy" question compared to one in which 10 per cent respond positively.

Given a choice situation involving these essential elements, the response of any given individual to an issue will be determined by the relation of his own position on the continuum to the point at which the issue intersects the continuum. From a knowledge of the individual's place on the continuum, we can predict his response pattern to the three issues. This relationship between response pattern and segment is shown in Table VI-2[3]

If the issue cuts the continuum to the right of a respondent's own position on the continuum, he will respond negatively. If the issue cuts the continuum to the left of his own position, the respondent will respond positively. Thus, any given individual will respond positively up to the point at which the issues begin to intersect the continuum to the right of his own position, and he will then respond negatively to the remainder. If all the issues cut the continuum to the right of his position, he will, of course, respond negatively to all of them; and if all the issues cut the continuum to the left of his position, he will respond positively to all of them.

Table VI-2

RELATIONSHIP BETWEEN RESPONSE PATTERN AND SEGMENT

Segment in Which Legislator Is Located	Number of Postitive Responses	Votes on Issues Whose Cutting Point Is:		
		c_1	c_2	c_3
A	0	—	—	—
B	1	+	—	—
C	2	+	+	—
D	3	+	+	+

The voting on a set of issues generates the pattern described above because a set does involve a response to a single variable. This pattern is called a scale or scalar pattern of response. If a set of issues involves responses to two or more variables, it is highly unlikely that the votes on the set will fall into a scalar pattern.

Imagine that we ask legislators:

    1. Are you six feet or over?
    2. Do you weigh at least 175 pounds?
    3. Are you a redhead?

What sort of pattern would we expect to observe in their responses? We can reasonably expect to see legislators distributed over all the possible response patterns as in Table VI-3.

Table VI-3

Question 1	Question 2	Question 3
Yes	Yes	Yes
Yes	Yes	No
Yes	No	No
No	No	No
Yes	No	Yes
No	Yes	No
No	No	Yes
No	Yes	Yes

We expect this because the three questions do not relate to a single variable. Each question relates to a different variable: one, to height; two, to weight; and three, to hair color. We have no reason to believe that these three variables will be highly correlated with each other. In such a case, we say that the three questions do not scale. Responses to the questions are not confined to the cumulative patterns, e.g., Yes, Yes, Yes; Yes, Yes, No, as would be the case if the three questions were cutting a common underlying continuum or a single dimension.

Applied to roll-call data, Guttman scaling involves an examination of the pattern of votes on a series of roll calls. If this pattern is scalar, or if it closely approximates a scalar pattern, we say that the votes scale and, hence, that the set provides a measure of a single variable.

We can distinguish two ways of using Guttman scaling in roll-call analysis. In the first type of analysis, the researcher begins by selecting from a population of roll calls one or more sets of roll calls that he believes share a common content. These sets are termed *preliminary universes of content*. Once the universes have been constructed, the roll calls in them are tested for scalability. In the second type of analysis, the researcher does not categorize votes into preliminary universes, but tests all the roll calls within a population for scalability and then selects from the mass those sets of roll calls which analysis reveals to be scalar. Although the two types of analysis involve similar procedures, enough differences between them occur that separate treatment is warranted.

ANALYSES BEGINNING WITH PRELIMINARY UNIVERSES[4]

We have noted that a preliminary universe is simply a set of roll calls that the investigator believes to be related to one another. To create a preliminary universe of content, the researcher examines a population of roll calls and classes together those votes that he believes share a common content. He does this on the basis of his knowledge of the substance of the roll calls and on the basis of any information he has gleaned from reading the debates that preceded the votes or from examining the context in which the votes were taken.

The total population of roll calls will probably yield several different universes of content, with a varying number of roll calls included in each. An example is found in the scale analysis study Duncan MacRae, Jr., conducted of the U.S. House of Representatives in the 81st Congress.[5] MacRae constructed from the roll calls of that Congress the universes in Table VI-4.

TABLE VI-4

1. Welfare state and domestic communism issues	60	roll calls
2. Agriculture and urban-rural issues	14	" "
3 Civil rights, Republican-Southern Democratic coalition, FEPC, etc.	24	" "
4. Other non-local domestic issues	22	" "
5. Mineral resources	8	" "
6. Appropriations, not otherwise classified	9	" "
7. Other and smaller domestic issues (including issues of local concern)	41	" "
8. Tariff and foreign affairs	36	" "
9. Military affairs	12	" "
10. Veterans' affairs	8	" "

If the researcher is interested in only one type of roll call, such as social welfare, he will construct only one preliminary universe of content. In such a case, he will examine his total population of roll calls for votes that he believes belong to a universe of social-welfare issues and ignore the remaining votes.

CONVERTING YEAS AND NAYS INTO POSITIVE AND NEGATIVE RESPONSES

Once roll calls have been classified into preliminary universes, "yea" and "nay" votes must be converted into positive and negative responses. This involves determining for each roll call the meaning of a "yea" or "nay" relevant to the variable being analyzed. In the illustration we have been using, "social welfare programs," the researcher determines for each roll call whether a "yea" or a "nay" vote actually constitutes a vote in support of "social welfare."

DETERMINING THE MARGINAL FREQUENCIES OF THE VOTES

When "yeas" and "nays" are converted into positive and negative responses, the researcher must determine the marginal frequencies of each vote. This is simply the percentage of legislators casting "positive" votes.

ORDERING THE VOTES IN TERMS OF MARGINAL FREQUENCIES

The votes should be ordered according to marginal frequencies when these have been established. Votes can be ordered from the most positive to the least positive, or the reverse. In this discussion, we shall assume that the votes are ordered in terms of marginal frequencies from the most to the least positive.

A careful record should be kept of each of these first four steps. This record should provide the following data:

1. A description of the content of each vote included in each universe.
2. A reference to where each vote can be found in the source document the researcher is using.
3. Comments on each vote that the researcher makes as he records the votes. Such comments can prove useful in interpreting the scales that are subsequently constructed.
4. An indication of what constitutes a positive vote.
5. The marginal frequency of each vote, i.e., the proportion of legislators voting who vote positively.
6. If the researcher is using data-processing equipment, an identification of the vote's deck and column number.

Table VI-5 illustrates one possible format for keeping such a record. The data are hypothetical roll calls taken in the U.S. House of Representatives. At the top of the form, the universe is identified. On the lefthand side of the page is noted the place in the source document at which the vote can be found. In this illustration, the document is the *Congressional Record*. Next, the content of each vote included in the universe is described. Although in the illustration this description is very brief, it is wise to provide a more complete and detailed description of the votes. Next, the "positive" vote is indicated for each roll

TABLE VI-5

HYPOTHETICAL DEMOCRAT LIBERALISM-CONSERVATISM UNIVERSE

Congressional Record Session and Page Number	Content of Roll Call	Positive Vote	Per Cent Voting Positively	Comments	IBM Identification
1-14673	Social Security Extension; consideration of bill	Y	.90		
1-15571	Public Housing; motion to recommit	N	.89		
1-14675	Social Security Extension; to consider resolution making in order	Y	.89		
1-27310	Internal Revenue Act Amendment; consideration	N	.60		
2-16789	Education Facilities Act; motion to recommit	N	.57		
2-21345	National Defense Emergency Act; consideration	N	.55		
2-22445	Resolution providing additional funds for Committee on Un-American Activities	N	.40		
2-31445	Defense Industry Subsidization Act; consideration	N	.32		
2-31448	Vocational Education Act; motion to amend	N	.10		

call. Following this, the proportion of legislators casting positive votes is indicated. Finally, space is left in which the researcher may record any comments or notes he wishes to keep on each vote, and space is provided for indicating the deck and column in which the vote is to be found in the researcher's punch-card file.

CROSS-TABULATING VOTES AGAINST EACH OTHER

When the researcher has completed the first four steps, he is ready to check the scalability of the votes he has included in a preliminary universe: that is, he is ready to determine which of the votes included do in fact belong to a common universe. Several methods have been developed for doing this. These include the scalogram board, the Cornell technique, and pairwise comparison of items.[6] We shall describe only the last method, pairwise comparison of items, because it appears to be the most appropriate of the three for constructing scales from roll-call data.

The pairwise comparison of items involves comparing one roll call against another roll call to determine the frequency of each of the four possible combinations of votes (absences being excluded). This procedure consists of cross-tabulating the votes on one roll call against the votes on another. The cross-tabulation results in a fourfold table (as in Figure VI-1) that shows the frequency of the four possible combinations of responses.

FIGURE VI-1

Roll Call 2

		+	−
Roll Call 1	+	a $++$	b $+-$
	−	c $-+$	d $--$

Cell *a* shows the number of legislators voting positively on both roll calls. Cell *b* shows the number of legislators casting a positive vote on the first roll call and a negative vote on the second. Cell *c* shows the number of voters casting a negative vote on vote 1 but a positive vote on vote 2. Cell *d* shows the number casting negative votes on both vote 1 and vote 2.

Ideally, each vote included in a universe should be cross-tabulated against all other votes. If a computer is not available, then the researcher can legitimately cross-tabulate each vote against the next five votes. (Remember that the votes in the universe have been ordered in marginal frequencies from the most to the least positive.) In the preliminary universe used in the illustration, nine roll calls are ranked, from one on which 90 per cent of the legislators cast a "positive" vote to one in which only 10 per cent voted "positive." In this case, we would cross-tabulate the first roll call against the next five roll calls, the second against the next five, the third against the next five, and so on through the series as in Table VI-6. This tabulation results in a series of 30 fourfold tables.

TABLE VI-6

Roll Calls

	1 X	2,3,4,5,6
	2 X	3,4,5,6,7
	3 X	4,5,6,7,8
Roll Calls	4 X	5,6,7,8,9
	5 X	6,7,8,9
	6 X	7,8,9
	7 X	8,9
	8 X	9

The cross-tabulation of votes and the construction of the fourfold tables can be done on a counter-sorter, particularly if the universe to be checked for scalability is small. Even then, however, the process is tedious. An IBM 101 Statistical Sorter is an excellent instrument for cross-tabulating because it can easily be wired and operated. A computer also can be employed, and its use, as will be clear in a moment, has important advantages.

DEFINING AND DETERMINING SCALABILITY

The fourfold tables generated by the cross-tabulation of votes become the basic data for determining the scalability of the votes included in the preliminary universes. The next steps in the analysis are to define scalability operationally and then to determine which votes in a universe conform to the criterion. This would be simple if the votes included in a universe formed a perfect scale. They would do so if in the fourfold tables only cells *a, b,* and *d* were filled and cell *c* were always vacant, as in the following illustration:

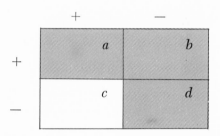

Cell *c*, which shows the frequency of legislators who cast a negative vote on the first roll call but a positive vote on the second roll call, is called the non-scale cell. The response pattern — + is the pattern we would not expect if the two items tapped a common dimension. For example, in our illustration using height as a variable, we would not expect a person to respond negatively to the question: "Are you 5 feet or more in height?" and then respond positively to the harder question: "Are you 6 feet or more in height?"

In reality, perfect scalability is rare, and some error can be permitted before concluding that two roll calls do not belong to a common universe. Because of this imperfection, the researcher must determine how much error he is willing to accept and still treat votes as scalar. Essentially, this is a problem of determining how large a frequency the non-scale cell (cell *c*) can have before the researcher must conclude that the votes in question do not scale or tap a common dimension. This determination can be made in at least three ways.

A *Simple Per Cent.* The simplest criterion of scalability is a designation of an absolute ceiling of error for all votes in a series.[7] The researcher may, for example, set this figure at 10 per cent. If less than 10 per cent of the voters (10 per cent of N) fall into the non-scale cell (the $-+$ cell), the two votes are deemed to scale with one another. If this ceiling is exceeded—if the non-scale cell contains more than 10 per cent of the voters—then the two votes are considered non-scalar. In Figure VI-2 below, votes 1 and 2 are non-scalar, while votes 1 and 3 are scalar.

FIGURE VI-2

		Vote 2						Vote 3		
		+	−					+	−	
Vote 1	+	.25	.25	.50		Vote 1	+	.42	.08	.50
	−	.25	.25	.50			−	.08	.42	.50
		.50	.50					.50	.50	
		$N = 100$						$N = 100$		

The level of permissible error is rather arbitrarily designated in this procedure. It could be 10 per cent, as in our illustration. It might be 5 per cent. The level of permissible error will depend on what sort of risks the researcher wishes to take. By setting the criterion of scalability high (say, at 3 per cent), he risks excluding votes that might belong to his universe. The researcher using this procedure to define scalability will consider what kind of scale he wishes and the uses he wishes to make of it before deciding upon a level of permissible error.

The designation of a simple per cent of permissible error is the simplest method of defining scalability, but it is by no means entirely satisfactory. In effect, this method assumes that the probability of error is constant throughout a series of votes, regardless of the size of their marginals. This assumption is not warranted. This objection, combined with others that need not concern us here, has led to the development of several alternative procedures for defining scalability.

The Exponential Model.   Duncan MacRae, Jr., has devised what is termed an exponential model for assessing fourfold tables and for determining the level of permissible error in the relation of two items. Because the model is relatively complex, its mathematical formulations will not be reviewed here. The reader is referred to "An Exponential Model for Assessing Fourfold Tables," *Sociometry*, 19 (June, 1956), 84-94. In this model, in contrast to a simple, absolute tolerance limit, the level of permissible error varies with the difference in the marginal frequencies of two votes and with the proportion of positive votes. In addition, the model contains a parameter, k, to which the researcher may assign a value. This permits him to vary, as his purposes may dictate, the general level of error to be tolerated in the relation of votes. As noted, the model is relatively complex and may at first seem difficult; but when it has been worked through and understood, it can be used easily and quickly.

Yule's Q.   Yule's Q provides an alternative method of assessing the scalability of pairs of roll calls. It has the advantage of being less complex than the exponential model, and it yields highly comparable results.[8] When Yule's Q is used, pairs of roll calls are cross-tabulated in fourfold tables, as described above (see Figure VI-3).

FIGURE VI-3

Roll Call 2

		+	—
	+	a	b
Roll Call 1			
	—	c	d

Yule's Q provides a measure of association between the pairs of votes.

$$Q = \frac{(ad - bc)}{(ad + bc)}$$

The value of Q ranges from -1.0 to 1.0. The higher the Q value, the greater the association or scalability of the roll calls. Thus, if two votes are perfectly scalar, for example:

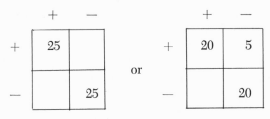

then $Q = 1.0$. If two votes are not related at all, for example:

	+	−
+	10	10
−	10	10

then $Q = 0.0$.

Using the Q formula, the researcher can calculate rapidly the relationship between each pair of votes. He can then specify a minimum value of Q and will deem any pair of votes falling below that value to be non-scalar. This value (Qmin.) will be determined by the researcher's purposes and needs. If scales with very little error are desired, then the value should be set high, perhaps at .8 or .9. If the investigator is willing to admit more error into the scale, he would set the value lower, perhaps at .6 or even .5.

DETERMINING THE ROLL CALLS THAT SCALE

Once the researcher has decided how he will define scalability, he examines the pairs of roll calls to determine which of them meet his definition and which do not. For example, in our illustration of the nine liberalism-conservatism votes, we would examine each of the thirty fourfold tables to determine which of the thirty pairs of votes conform to the criteria of scalability. Normally, the results of such an examination will look something like Table VI-7.

TABLE VI-7

1 X ②,3,④,⑤,6
2 X   3,④,⑤,6,⑦
3 X   4,5,⑥,⑦,8
4 X   ⑤,⑥,⑦,8,⑨
5 X   ⑥,⑦,8,⑨
6 X   7,⑧,9
7 X   8,⑨
8 X   ⑨

The numbers circled show the pairs of votes that meet a specified definition of scalability. The uncircled numbers are pairs that fail to scale. Thus, in the illustration we see that vote 1 scales with votes 2, 4, and 5 but fails to scale with votes 3 and 6. Vote 2 scales with 4, 5, and 7 but does not scale with votes 3 and 6. On the basis of this information about the pairs of votes, we can select from the total universe of votes the particular votes that constitute a scalable subset of votes within the universe. In our illustration, we observe a subset of six votes, votes 1, 2, 4, 5, 7, and 9. These votes are all mutually scalar. The remaining votes, 3, 6, and 8, scale with some but not all of the other six votes. A vote to be included in a scale must scale with all other votes; since 3, 6, and 8 do not, they are excluded from the scalable subset.

The votes that are excluded from a scalable subset should be examined to see if together they may form another distinct or partially distinct scalable subset. When this is done in our example, we find that votes 3 and 6 scale, as do votes 6 and 8; but vote 3 does not scale with vote 8. Had vote 3 and vote 8 scaled, we would have had a second scalable subset of votes within the universe, in addition to the large subset of six votes that we identified initially.

CHECKING VOTES AGAINST ROLL CALLS INCLUDED
IN OTHER UNIVERSES

After the preliminary universes of votes have been checked for scalability and the scalable subsets of votes have been determined in each universe, these subsets of votes should be checked against votes that are included in other universes. The criteria for including or excluding a particular vote from a particular universe are largely subjective, and the researcher's judgment may be in error as far as the empirical facts are concerned. It is possible that votes initially classified in one universe may in fact scale with votes initially classified in a different universe. Thus, it is wise for the researcher to check the validity of his subjective judgments by comparing votes from different universes. This will be done in the manner in which the votes in preliminary universes are checked with one another. One vote is cross-tabulated against another, and the resulting fourfold-table data are assessed in terms of the scalability of the pairs of votes. If this search turns up additional votes that scale with one another and with votes already included in a scalable subset, the set will be expanded to include the additional items.

CONSTRUCTING SCALES

Once he has determined the scalable votes within a universe and has checked them against other votes initially classified in other universes, the researcher is ready to construct from the scalable subset of votes an actual scale.

First, he examines the votes in the scalable subsets to determine if any of them can be combined to form a contrived item—that is, a cutting point for the scale that consists of two or more roll calls.[9] This can be done when two votes are identical, or nearly so, in marginal frequencies. In our illustration, six votes comprise the scalable subset: votes 1, 2, 4, 5, 7, and 9. The marginal frequencies of these votes are:

1	.90
2	.89
4	.60
5	.57
7	.40
9	.10

We can combine votes 1 and 2 to form a contrived item for our scale. We can also combine votes 4 and 5 to form such an item, because their marginal frequencies are almost the same. A cross-tabulation of votes 1 and 2 might look like Figure VI-4.

FIGURE VI-4

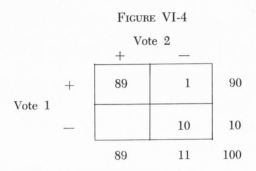

All but one legislator who voted positively on vote 1 also voted positively on vote 2. In short, the two votes are for all practical purposes carbon copies of one another. Hence, we combine them. The same is true of votes 4 and 5.

Invariably, a number of legislators are absent or for other reasons do not vote on any given roll call. By combining two or more highly similar votes into a common item, we can partially solve the absence problem. A legislator absent on one of the roll calls in a contrived item may vote on the other roll calls making up the item and, hence, can be placed on the scale by his response to these votes.

We now have a scale consisting of two contrived items and two items representing single roll calls. Scale item one is a combination of votes 1 and 2. Scale item two is a combination of votes 4 and 5. Scale item three is vote 7. Scale item four is vote 9. Recalling our earlier discussion of the nature of Guttman scales, we can conceptualize this scale as four items cutting a continuum at four different points.

Item 1   Item 2   Item 3   Item 4

PLACING LEGISLATORS IN SCALE TYPES

After a scale has been constructed, scale types can be assigned to legislators. This can be done according to the instructions that follow.

A. List the responses of the legislators to the votes comprising the scale. The listing will resemble Table VI-8.

TABLE VI-8

Legislator	Item 1		Item 2		Item 3	Item 4
	(Vote 1	Vote 2)	(Vote 4	Vote 5)	(Vote 7)	(Vote 9)
A	+	+	+	+	+	+
B	+	—	—	—	—	—
C	+	+	+	+	—	—
D	+	+	O	O	O	—
E	+	+	+	+	+	—
F	—	—	—	—	—	—
G	—	—	—	—	+	—
H	—	—	+	+	—	+
I	+	+	O	O	—	—
J	+	+	—	—	+	—

B. Determine the legislators' responses on contrived items. This involves combining a legislator's responses on the votes comprising the item and deriving from them a "positive" or "negative" classification on the contrived items. This is easily done when a legislator votes in the same way on all the roll calls comprising a contrived item. In our illustration, for example, Legislator A casts a positive vote on both roll calls comprising contrived item one. He is thus assigned a positive response for the contrived item. Legislator F casts a negative vote on both roll calls comprising item one. He is therefore assigned a negative response for the contrived item. Normally, this will not be the case for all legislators. In the above illustration, Legislator B votes positively on vote 1 but negatively on vote 2. His response on the contrived item is thus + —. How is he classified on the contrived item? No absolute rule by which to decide this kind of case is available, but a rule of thumb can be followed. When a tie exists for a contrived item, the item is assigned whatever value (+ or −) will move it closer to the scale type containing the median case. This keeps the extreme scale types pure. Thus, in our illustration we would assign a "positive" to the contrived item. We have thus moved Legislator B toward the center of the continuum, keeping the extreme, all-negative response type pure.

In the case of contrived items composed of more than two votes, a legislator can be typed on the item according to his most frequent response. For example, on a contrived item composed of three votes, a legislator voting + − + would be typed + on the contrived item. If there is a tie (e.g., −, O, +), then the rule of thumb given above is employed.

We now have a scale and the pattern of responses described in Table VI-9.

TABLE VI-9

Legislator	Scale Item 1	Scale Item 2	Scale Item 3	Scale Item 4	Scale Score
A	+	+	+	+	4
B	+	−	−	−	1
C	+	+	−	−	2
D	+	O	O	−	NC*
E	+	+	+	−	3
F	−	−	−	−	0
G	−	−	+	−	0**
H	−	+	−	+	NC**
I	+	O	−	−	2*
J	+	−	+	−	2

C. Determine the number of "positive" responses for legislators with perfect scale patterns. The number of his positive responses is the legislator's scale type. Thus, Legislator A, having four positive responses, is assigned a scale score of 4; Legislator B, a scale score of 1; Legislator C, a scale score of 2; Legislator E, a scale score of 3; and Legislator F, a scale score of 0.

D. Determine the scale assignment of legislators with non-perfect scale patterns. These non-perfect patterns will be of two kinds: patterns displaying absences or non-responses; and patterns displaying non-scalar responses.

The treatment of non-responses. Several rules of thumb have been developed to deal with response patterns containing non-responses. (1) If a legislator fails to respond on one-half or more of the votes, he is not assigned a scale position. (In reporting the results of a scale, such individuals would be listed as not classified by the scale.) (2) In the case of all other absences, all possible scale positions are listed and the average scale position is then determined. The legislator can be assigned this scale type. When an average falls halfway between two scale types, the legislator should be assigned the one closest to the median of the scale. Legislator I has the following response pattern: $+$, O, $-$, $-$. He could be assigned to scale type 2 ($+$, $+$, $-$, $-$) or to scale type 1 ($+$, $-$, $-$, $-$). Since the average scale type comes halfway between these two, he is assigned to the scale type that is nearest to the median of the scale. This could be either scale type 1 or type 2, depending on the distribution of legislators on the scale.

The treatment of non-scale responses. No absolute rules exist for dealing with non-scale types. The following rules are suggested: (1) Legislators casting more than one non-scale vote normally should not be classified on the scale. Legislator H falls into this category. (This rule, of course, is dependent on the number of items in the scale and on the researcher's purposes. It may be modified as the situation appears to warrant. The important point is that the researcher explicitly indicate what rule he is following and communicate this clearly to the readers of his report.) (2) In all other cases, legislators casting non-scale votes can be typed in the following ways: (a) Error should be assigned to the vote that would result in a perfect scale type. In our illustration, Legislator G votes $-$, $-$, $+$, $-$. We would correct this error by changing his response on item 3 to a negative response, thus creating a perfect scale type, $-$, $-$, $-$, $-$. (b) When the error can be corrected in one of two ways to produce a perfect scale type, the legislator should be assigned the mean scale score between the two. Thus, in our illustration, Legislator *J* votes +, —, +, —. We could assign the error to item 2 or to item 3. If we assign it to item 2, *J* would have a scale position 3; if we assign it to item 3, he would have a scale position 1. The average of these two possible corrections is 2. Again, when the mean falls midway between two scale types, the legislator should be assigned the scale type closest to the scale position containing the median case.

E. List the scale type assignments for each legislator. In the table on page 108, these assignments are shown as scale scores. Note the asterisks on the corrected and on the non-classified scale scores. The researcher should keep a record and should communicate to his readers the fact that the classification into scale type of some legislators was made on the basis of corrections. In our illustration, a single asterisk beside a scale score indicates that the legislator's response contained some absences and the researcher had to make a scale assignment. The single asterisk beside the NC indicates that Legislator *D* was not classified on the scale because of an excess number of absences. The double asterisk indicates the presence of non-scale votes in the legislator's response pattern and shows that the researcher, following specified rules, has made a decision about the assignment of these legislators. The double asterisk following the NC indicates that the legislator was not classified by the scale because of the presence of an excess number of non-scale votes.

SUMMARIZING AND REPORTING SCALES

Scales can be summarized and reported in many ways. Table VI-10 shows one of these ways that is often convenient. On the extreme right of the table are identified the roll calls that were found to be mutually scalar. The next column shows the position of the roll calls on the scale moving downward from the "easiest" item to the "hardest." On the left are shown the distribution of scale positions or types and the number of legislators assigned to each type.

TABLE VI-10

DEMOCRATS: LIBERALISM-CONSERVATISM SCALE (HYPOTHETICAL)

Scale Type	Number Placed in Scale Type	Item Number	Identification	
0	2	1	(1-14673)	Social Security Extension; consideration of the bill (Y)
1	1		(1-15571)	Public Housing; motion to recommit (N)
2	3	2	(1-27310)	Internal Revenue Act; amendment (N)
			(2-16789)	Education Facilities Act; motion to recommit (N)
3	1	3	(2-22445)	Resolution providing additional funds for the Committee on Un-American Activities (N)
4	1	4	(2-31448)	Vocational Education Act; motion to amend (N)
Not classified	2			
Total	10			

APPRAISING THE ADEQUACY OF THE SCALE

The final step in scale construction is appraisal of the adequacy of the scale. Conventionally, a scale is appraised in terms of its reproducibility. The coefficient of reproducibility measures the proportion of responses on the scale items that could be predicted correctly from a knowledge of the legislator's scale scores or position. This coefficient is determined by dividing the number of correct responses by the total number of responses. The ambiguous-response scale responses—that is, response patterns that contained absences—can be eliminated from this calculation. Thus, in our illustration we would eliminate from our calculations the responses of Legislators *D* and *I*. We thus have eight legislators responding to four items. This gives us a total of 32 responses. Of these 32 responses, 4 are non-scale votes. Legislator *G* cast 1; Legislator *H*, 2; and Legislator *J*, 1. This leaves a total of 28 correct responses out of the 32 responses. Dividing the correct responses (28) by the number of total responses (32) yields a coefficient of reproducibility of .875. This means, in effect, that in 87.5 per cent of the cases we could accurately predict the legislators' responses to the scale items on the basis of a knowledge of their scale scores.

Conventionally, .90 has been considered a floor below which a scale's reproducibility cannot fall before it must be considered inadequate. The scale in our illustration does not quite meet this conventional standard. Whether the researcher accepts the scale or not will depend upon his purposes. Again, the important point is that he make explicit what he is doing and communicate it to his audience. In every instance, he should take care to report the reproducibility of his scales (or some other index of adequacy or error). In most cases, scales constructed by the procedures we have outlined will have a high level of reproducibility if the researcher sets his criteria of scalability at a reasonable level.

ANALYSIS NOT BEGINNING WITH
PRELIMINARY UNIVERSES

Most studies of legislative voting using Guttman scaling procedures have involved the type of analysis just discussed, in which the researcher first selects one or more preliminary universes of roll calls judged to share a common content and then proceeds to examine the scalability of votes within the universes. The researcher's judgment can err in the initial selection of roll calls for a universe, and even a careful checking of roll calls in one scalable subset against roll calls initially classified in other universes does not guarantee that errors will be avoided entirely. Even though he takes precautions, the researcher

. . . may fail to group issues as the legislators did, or even ignore certain issues. Moreover, in searching for issues or attitudes he might overlook certain bloc divisions that were not easily identifiable by common issue content, but could nevertheless be revealed by the same procedures.[10]

Duncan MacRae, Jr., has developed scaling procedures that do not entail the classification of roll calls into issue groups as the initial step in scale analysis.[11] A complete description of these procedures is beyond the limits of this book, but we will outline their major features.

THE CALCULATION OF Q-COEFFICIENTS FOR PAIRS OF ROLL CALLS

By MacRae's method, every roll call in the population of roll calls being studied is compared with every other roll call. Yule's Q is used to measure the association between each pair.[12] A minimum value for Q is specified. Each pair of votes is then classified as "scalable" or "not scalable," depending on whether the Q value of the pair attains the specified minimum.

THE PLACEMENT OF Q VALUES IN A MATRIX

The Q values of pairs of votes classified as "scalable" are then represented in a matrix. This matrix of Q values becomes the basis for identifying clusters of mutually scalable roll calls. Figure VI-5 is a reproduction of a Q-matrix constructed by MacRae for Republicans in the U.S. House of Representatives in the 84th Congress, 1955-1956.[13]

On each row and its corresponding column, a roll call is identified by the year in which it was taken and by the number that the *Congressional Quarterly* assigned to the vote. In the 84th Congress, 102 roll calls occurred on which the Republican party members split by at least seven to ninety-three per cent. MacRae, for reasons of space, displays in this matrix only the 31 roll calls that form scalable clusters. (A minimum value of $Q =$ 0.8 was used in this study. The Q values in the matrix have been multiplied by 10.) MacRae defined as "positive" the vote associated with the Republican party, as contrasted with that common among the Democrats. (There is one exception to this, and the vote is marked in the table with a dagger.)

The matrix reveals the sets of mutually scalable votes. These are sets all of whose pairs have association of at least .8. MacRae has indicated these sets or clusters by enclosing the votes in boxes.

The largest cluster of votes designated by "1" consists of eight roll calls. Of these, seven related to foreign aid and one to the matter of debt limits. MacRae discovered that the debate on debt limits included reference to foreign aid. (This discovery emphasizes that the researcher in interpreting the "meaning" of sets of scalable roll calls is well advised to supplement his knowledge of the roll calls within the scale by reference to as much additional information about them as is available to him.) The next two largest clusters ("2" and "3") include seven roll calls each. The votes in "2" dealt with agricultural issues, and the votes in "3" related to reciprocal trade. The smaller sets ("4" and "5") dealt with the pay of postal employees and with housing and atomic power respectively.

When clusters or sets of mutually scalable roll calls have been identified, these roll calls can be organized into scales, and legislators' scale positions can be determined by following the procedures described in the previous section.

AN ILLUSTRATION OF THE USE OF GUTTMAN SCALE ANALYSIS

Guttman scale analysis is highly useful in the study of legislative voting and is very widely used. Among the legislatures that have been studied through Guttman scaling are the American Congress, state legislatures, the British and French legislative assemblies, and the UN General Assembly.[14]

A longitudinal study of congressional voting on foreign aid done by Leroy Rieselbach provides an example of one use of the technique.[15] Rieselbach constructed scales of roll calls in the U.S. House of Representatives relating to foreign aid issues in each of five Congresses stretching from the 76th (1939-1940) to the 85th (1957-1958). On the basis of the legislators' scale scores, he classified legislators into three categories: "isolationists" ("those whose votes indicate a reluctance to expand the size or scope of the American foreign aid program"); "moderates"; and "internationalists" ("those who, by their votes, supported the maintenance of the program at the most extensive possible levels"). Rieselbach then analyzed these three groups of legislators in terms of party affiliation and three types of demographic variables.

First, the association of certain personal characteristics of the individual congressmen with their voting on foreign aid was examined. These attributes included educational attainment, occupation prior to election, religious affiliation, and prior service in the armed forces. Then, a set of "political" characteristics, including length of service in the House, committee service, and electoral margin, were related to votes on foreign aid. Finally, a number of constituency characteristics—region, ethnicity, ruralism, socioeconomic status, and educational level—were correlated with positions on the foreign aid issue.[16]

Table VI-11 shows the association between scale position and party in each of the five Congresses included in the study.[17]

TABLE VI-11

DISTRIBUTION OF REPRESENTATIVES
ON FOREIGN AID, BY PARTY AND CONGRESS

Party and voting position*	Congress				
	76th	77th	80th	83d	85th
Republicans	%	%	%	%	%
Isolationists	91.9	84.0	24.4	36.7	36.8
Internationalists	0.0	6.2	14.4	55.2	54.9
Democrats					
Isolationists	0.0	4.1	3.1	13.4	29.8
Internationalists	79.8	89.1	65.6	72.2	47.1

* For the sake of simplicity, the moderate groups, and those who were not scalable, are omitted from the table. Thus, the percentages for each party do not add to 100%. The percentage of moderates for each Congress is as follows: Republicans, 1,7, 8.6, 52.4, 4.5, 5.4; Democrats, 8.4, 0.0, 20.0, 11.1, 20.6. The percentages for the not scalable groups are: Republicans, 16.4, 1.2, 8.8, 3.6, 2.9; Democrats, 11.8, 6.7, 11.7, 3.2, 2.51. The latter category combines the non-scale types with those who could not be assigned because they were "on the record" too infrequently.

FIGURE VI-5

Q-MATRIX FOR REPUBLICANS, U.S. HOUSE OF REPRESENTATIVES, 84TH CONGRESS[*]

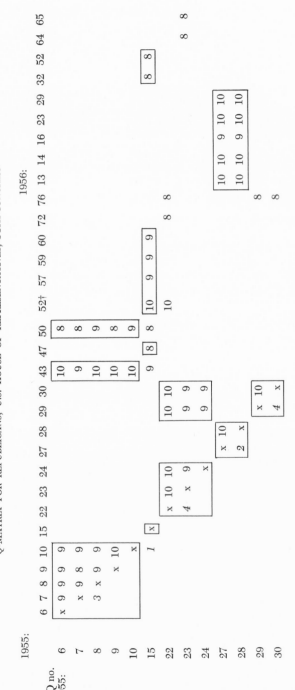

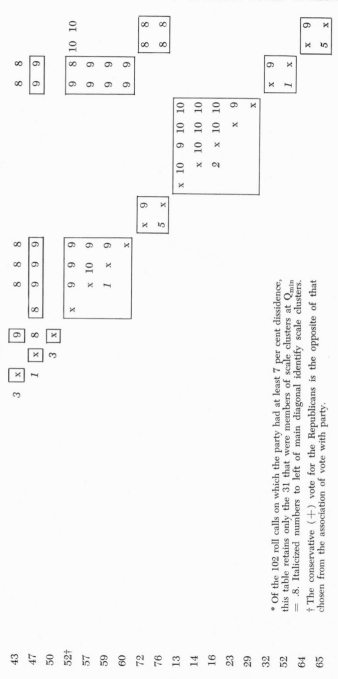

* Of the 102 roll calls on which the party had at least 7 per cent dissidence, this table retains only the 31 that were members of scale clusters at Q_{min} = .8. Italicized numbers to left of main diagonal identify scale clusters.

† The conservative (+) vote for the Republicans is the opposite of that chosen from the association of vote with party.

The table reveals a good deal of information about the structure of congressional voting over time. As Rieselbach observes:

> First, it shows that the collapse of party solidarity began before, rather than after World War II. Immediately after the 1940 election, a few Republicans crossed party lines to vote for an internationalist program while at the same time a handful of Democrats bolted and opposed Lend-Lease. Thus, while the war and the end of the Roosevelt era may have accelerated the change, the break-down of party unanimity cannot be attributed solely to these factors. Second, while the long-run development can be explained in terms of a number of factors—for example, the election of a Republican President, of an internationalist bent, which increased the pressures on G.O.P. legislators to back the foreign aid program; the simultaneous decline in the effectiveness of pulls from the executive on the Democrats; and the changing character of the American South which in turn led to increased fiscal conservatism and isolationism among representatives of that region—the important point here is that with the passage of time the importance of single variables as correlates of voting behavior may ebb and flow. Specifically in this case, party was of considerably less importance as a determinant of foreign aid voting in the 85th Congress than it had been 20 years earlier.[18]

By following procedures similar to those used in examining the relationship between party and scale position, Rieselbach analyzed also the association between legislators' position on the "isolationist-internationalist" dimension and the three types of demographic variables mentioned above.

Not only does Rieselbach's study illustrate the use of Guttman scale analysis in studying the relationship between voting patterns and factors believed to affect these patterns, but it also emphasizes an important fact about roll-call analysis. Roll-call studies can consume large amounts of time and resources. Often, the researcher confines his analysis to one session of a legislative body. He may succeed in isolating apparently significant relationships between voting behavior and one or more characteristics of the legislators studied. He is tempted to generalize from his findings: to assume that what is true at one time will be equally true in other time periods. While this may be true, the researcher should exercise caution in matters of inference here as elsewhere in roll-call research. Rieselbach's findings reveal one good reason for this: The types of factors that most significantly affect voting patterns change over periods of time. As he concludes, "a large number of variables of different types interacting with the political situation of the moment produce a vote configuration which alters with the passage of time".[19] While this constitutes good reason for caution about generalizing findings, it is not reason to despair. Political change in one of the most significant social phenomena that political scientists can study systematically and, as the Rieselbach research illustrates, roll-call analysis provides one means of examining political change.

A NOTE ON THE NATURE OF THE DIMENSIONS OF VOTING IDENTIFIED THROUGH GUTTMAN SCALE ANALYSIS

The conceptual meaning of the scalar patterns in voting revealed by the procedures discussed in this chapter is by no means clear. On the whole, political scientists have treated these patterns as psychological phenomena, seeing scalable dimensions as attitudinal in nature or immediate origin. Although such a conceptualization may be adequate for most purposes, it probably is an oversimplification of the phenomena observed. Some evidence exists that scalar patterns are not simply continua in attitude structure or frames of reference. Scalar patterns appear to be highly complex features of legislative voting behavior, features that are conditioned by an interaction of situational and organizational as well as psychological variables.[20]

NOTES

[1] S. A. Stouffer, *et al., Measurement and Prediction* (Princeton, N.J.: Princeton University Press, 1950).

[2] The essential elements of the discussion of Guttman scaling theory and procedures are freely borrowed from Duncan MacRae, Jr., *Dimensions of Congressional Voting* (Berkeley: University of California Press, 1958). MacRae has pioneered the development of roll-call analysis in recent years. His work on and use of Guttman scaling has been especially innovative and has greatly influenced the research of many students of roll-call voting, including the authors

of this handbook. To say that this particular chapter could not have been written without the work MacRae has done on the application of Guttman scaling to roll-call analysis is to report a simple and very literal fact.

[3] The table and the figure used just before are taken from MacRae, p. 219.

[4] The procedures described were developed by MacRae. See particularly Appendix A of *Dimensions of Congressional Voting.*

[5] *Ibid.,* p. 317.

[6] See, respectively, Stouffer *et al., op. cit.,* Ch. IV; L. Guttman, "The Cornell Technique for Scale and Intensity Analysis," *Educational and Psychological Measurement,* 7 (Summer, 1947), 247-80; and J. Toby and M. L. Toby, "A Method of Selecting Dichotomous Items by Cross-Tabulation," Ch. XV in J. W. Riley, M. W. Riley, and J. Toby, *Sociological Studies in Scale Analysis* (New Brunswick, N.J.: Rutgers University Press, 1954).

[7] Toby and Toby, *op. cit.* For an example of research using this criterion, see David M. Wood, "Issue Dimensions in a Multi-Party System: The French National Assembly and European Unification," *Midwest Journal of Political Science,* 8 (August, 1964), 255-76.

[8] Duncan MacRae, Jr., "Intra-Party Division and Cabinet Coalitions in the Fourth French Republic," *Comparative Studies in Society and History,* 5 (January, 1963), 164-211. MacRae has developed a program for an IBM 1401 for computing Q coefficients. See "IBM 1401 Q-Matrix and Editing Programs for Legislative Votes," *Behavioral Science,* 10 (July, 1965), 324.

[9] This procedure was proposed by S. A. Stouffer, E. F. Borgatta, D. G. Hays, and A. F. Henry in "A Technique for Improving Cumulative Scales," *Public Opinion Quarterly,* 16 (Summer, 1952), 273-91.

[10] Duncan MacRae, Jr., "A Method for Identifying Issues and Factions from Legislative Votes," *American Political Science Review* 59 (December, 1965), 911.

[11] *Ibid.* See also MacRae, "Intra-Party Division and Cabinet Coalitions in the Fourth French Republic," *op. cit.*

[12] For a computer program for calculating Q coefficients, see MacRae, "IBM 1401 Q-Matrix and Editing Programs for Legislative Votes," *op. cit.*

[13] "A Method for Identifying Issues and Factions from Legislative Votes," *op. cit.,* p. 914.

[14] See MacRae, *Dimensions of Congressional Voting, op. cit.;* George M. Belknap, "A Method for Analyzing Legislative Behavior," *Midwest Journal of Political Science,* 2 (November, 1958), 377-402; Charles D. Farris, "A Method for Determining Ideological Groupings in the Congress," *Journal of Politics,* 20 (May, 1958), 308-38; Mark Kesselman, "Presidential Leadership in Congress in Foreign Policy," *Midwest Journal of Political Science,* 5 (August, 1961), 284-89;

Hugh D. Price, "Are Southern Democrats Different? An Application of Scale Analysis to Senate Voting Patterns," in Nelson W. Polsby, Robert A. Dentler, and Paul A. Smith (eds.), *Politics and Social Life* (Boston: Houghton Mifflin Company, 1963), pp. 740-56; Lee F. Anderson, "Variability in the Unidimensionality of Legislative Voting," *Journal of Politics*, 26 (August, 1964), 568-85; Lee F. Anderson, "Individuality in Voting in Congress: A Research Note," *Midwest Journal of Political Science*, 8 (November, 1964), 425-29; L. N. Rieselbach, "The Demography of the Congressional Vote on Foreign Aid, 1939-1958," *American Political Science Review*, 48 (September, 1964), 577-788; Samuel C. Patterson, "Dimensions of Voting Behavior in a One-Party Legislature," *Public Opinion Quarterly*, 26 (Summer, 1962), 185-200; Samuel C. Patterson, "Legislative Leadership and Political Ideology," *Public Opinion Quarterly*, 27 (Fall, 1963), 399-410; Duncan MacRae, Jr., "Roll Call Votes and Leadership," *Public Opinion Quarterly*, 20 (Fall, 1956), 543-58; MacRae, "Intra-Party Division and Cabinet Coalitions in the Fourth French Republic," *op. cit.*; David M. Wood, *op. cit.*; William O. Aydelotte, "Voting Patterns in the British House of Commons in the 1840's," *Comparative Studies in Society and History*, 5 (January, 1963), 134-63; Leroy N. Rieselbach, "Quantitative Techniques for Studying Voting Behavior in the U.N. General Assembly," *International Organization*, 14 (Spring, 1960), 291-306.

[15]Rieselbach, "The Demography of the Congressional Vote on Foreign Aid, 1939-1958," *op. cit.*

[16]Rieselbach, p. 578.

[17]*Ibid.*

[18]*Ibid.*, pp. 578-79.

[19]*Ibid.*, p. 588.

[20]Anderson, "Variability in the Unidimensionality of Legislative Voting," *op. cit.*

Guttman scaling techniques have been used widely in studies of judicial voting. The possibility was first suggested in a paper by Joseph Tanenhaus, "The Uses and Limitations of Social Science Methods in Analyzing Judicial Behavior" (Washington, D.C.: American Political Science Association, September 7, 1956, mimeographed). Significant illustrations of the use of Guttman scaling include Glendon Schubert, *Quantitative Analysis of Judicial Behavior* (Glencoe: The Free Press, 1959), Ch. 5; Sidney Ulmer, "Supreme Court Behavior and Civil Rights," *Western Political Quarterly*, 13 (June, 1960), 288-311; "Scaling Judicial Cases: A Methodological Note," *American Behavioral Scientist*, 4 (April, 1961), 31-34; "The Analysis of Behavior Patterns of the United States Supreme Court," *Journal of Politics*, 22 (1960), 629-53; and Glendon Schubert, *The Judicial Mind: The Attitude and Ideology of Supreme Court Justices* (Evanston, Ill.: Northwestern University Press, 1965).

CHAPTER VII

METHODS FOR SELECTING ROLL CALLS, DESCRIBING THE BEHAVIOR OF INDIVIDUAL LEGISLATORS, AND IDENTIFYING GROUPS OF LEGISLATORS: FACTOR ANALYSIS

We described Guttman scale analysis as one of two multi-purpose techniques commonly used in roll-call analysis. Factor analysis is the second of these.[1] Like Guttman scaling, factor analysis provides a means of describing roll calls and a means of describing the voting behavior of individual legislators and groups of legislators. The method determines, for a given number of variables (these may be either roll calls or legislators), a smaller number of "underlying dimensions," which are termed *factors*.

Like Guttman scale analysis, factor analysis was developed outside political science and has been borrowed and adapted by students of legislative behavior. Factor analysis has been used most extensively in psychology, in which countless such analyses have been performed in the search for "dimensions" of personality and mental ability.[2] The use of factor analysis on various types of social data is rapidly spreading, however, and its general applicability to the analysis of roll calls is being increasingly recognized.[3] As was noted above, factor analysis can be used to describe and measure variations among roll calls and to examine the voting behavior of individual legislators and of groups of legislators. In an early study, Carlson and Harrell analyzed 93 roll-call votes of 34 leading United States Representatives and Senators and obtained four factors or groupings of legislators.[4] Similarly, Chester Harris in a study of 95 senators on 9 roll calls found three factors.[5] In each of these cases, the positions of the legislators on the factors, as well as those of the empirical groups delimited, could be examined. In analyzing the two houses of the Kansas legislature (125 representatives on 41 votes, and 40 senators on 57 votes), John Grumm derived four factors for the Senate and five for the House.[6] In addition, he related variations in roll-call content to the obtained groupings of legislators. In a somewhat different design,[7] Hayward Alker factor-analyzed 70 United Nations roll calls to discover major dimensions of conflict. Through further analysis, he placed the nations on 6 voting dimensions and also related these individual positions to the commonly defined UN blocs.[8] These last two studies especially illustrate the versatility of factor analysis in relation to the basic inquiries of roll-call analysis. They demonstrate also how the results of factor analysis can usefully be linked to other relevant variables.

Factor analysis is the most complex method of roll-call analysis discussed in this book. Although complete description or discussion of the method is beyond the scope of this chapter, we shall describe essential features of factor theory and then illustrate a factor analysis using roll calls from the U.S. Senate.

FACTOR THEORY

Let us begin with a hypothetical data matrix having values or scores of M variables (personality traits, socioeconomic characteristics, roll calls) on N units (individuals, groups, cities, nations) as in Figure VII-1.[9]

FIGURE VII-1

VARIABLES

		1	2	3	.	.	.	M
	1	X_{11}	X_{12}	X_{13} .	.	.	.	X_{1m}
	2	X_{21}	X_{22}	X_{23} .	.	.	.	X_{2m}
U	3	X_{31}	X_{32}	X_{33} .	.	.	.	X_{3m}
N								
I	.	.	.	.				.
T								
S	.	.	.	.				.
	.	.	.	.				.
	N	X_{n1}	X_{n2}	X_{n3} .	.	.	.	X_{nm}

Each variable, taken over the N units, will show a certain amount of spread or variation, in that its value varies from unit to unit. A statistical expression of this variation is the *variance*, symbolized by σ^2.[10]

Now suppose, in addition, that we have obtained a set of correlations for these M variables, giving us the abstract correlation matrix in Figure VII-2.[11]

FIGURE VII-2

VARIABLES

		1	2	3	.	.	.	M
V	1	r_{11}	r_{12}	r_{13}	.	.	.	r_{1m}
A	2	r_{21}	r_{22}	r_{23}	.	.	.	r_{2m}
R								
I	3	r_{31}	r_{32}	r_{33}	.	.	.	r_{3m}
A								
B	.	.	.	.				.
L								
E	.	.	.	.				.
S	.	.	.	.				.
	M	r_{m1}	r_{m2}	r_{m3}	.	.	.	r_{mm}

Each correlation in the matrix, as a measure of the relationship between two variables, can be interpreted as expressing the amount of variance shared by those two variables.[12] The amount of shared variance is given by squaring the correlation value. For example, a correlation of .7 is equal to a shared variance of .49. This coefficient (r^2) is sometimes called the coefficient of determination. This interpretation is illustrated in Figure VII-3, in which the circles represent variance of the variables, and the shaded areas represent shared variance.

FIGURE VII-3

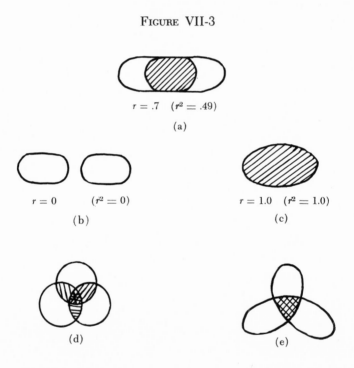

$r = .7$ ($r^2 = .49$)

(a)

$r = 0$ ($r^2 = 0$) $r = 1.0$ ($r^2 = 1.0$)

(b)   (c)

(d)   (e)

Figure VII-3(a) is equivalent to the example given above in which a correlation of .7 is equal to a shared variance of .49. Figure VII-3(b) presents the case of two variables sharing *no* variance; and Figure VII-3(c), the case of variables having *all* their variance in common. The configurations in (d) and (e) are alternative representations of the variance shared among *three* variables. Diagrams such as these, of course, become exceedingly complex as variables are added. Factor analysis, then, assumes that the correlation matrix contains or is permeated by a complex configuration of shared variance that can be expressed in terms of a limited number of *common factors*, each of which represents a portion of the total variance. The shaded portion of Figure VII-3(e), for example, represents a common factor underlying the intercorrelations of those three variables. In this conception, a variable is thought of as comprising three variance components, which, when added together, comprise the total variance (σ^2) of that variable. These are:

> *common variance (communality)*—the portion of the total error-free variance that correlates with the other variables.
>
> *specific variance (specificity)*—the portion of the total error-free variance that does not correlate with any of the other variables.
>
> *error variance*—the portion of the total variance that results from all influences contributing to unreliability (sampling error, measurement error, changes within the unit, etc.).

By combining these types of variance, we can derive two additional types that are of theoretical importance:

> *reliable variance (reliability)*—common and specific variance combined (excluding all variance due to error).
>
> *unique variance (uniqueness)*—specific and error variance combined (excluding all variance held in common with other variables).

We can thus represent the total variance of a variable, j, by the following equation:

$$\sigma_j^2 = \underbrace{\sigma_{j1}^2 + \sigma_{j2}^2 + \ldots + \sigma_{jr}^2}_{} + \underbrace{\sigma_{js}^2}_{} + \underbrace{\sigma_{je}^2}_{} \quad (1)$$

$$\begin{array}{ccccc} \text{total} & & \text{common} & + & \text{specific} + \text{error} \\ \text{variance} & = & \text{variances} & & \text{variance} \ \ \text{variance} \end{array}$$

By dividing both sides of this equation by σ_j^2, we put it in standard form:

$$\frac{\sigma_j^2}{\sigma_j^2} = 1.0 = \frac{\sigma_{j1}^2}{\sigma_j^2} + \frac{\sigma_{j2}^2}{\sigma_j^2} + \ldots + \frac{\sigma_{jr}^2}{\sigma_j^2} + \frac{\sigma_{js}^2}{\sigma_j^2} + \frac{\sigma_{je}^2}{\sigma_j^2} \quad (2)$$

For ease of presentation, each type of variance will be given a symbol; and equation (2) can then be rewritten as follows:[13]

$$1.0 = \underbrace{a_{j1}^2 + a_{j2}^2 + \ldots + a_{jr}^2}_{\substack{\text{common} \\ \text{variances}}} + \underbrace{s_j^2}_{\substack{\text{specific} \\ \text{variance}}} + \underbrace{e_j^2}_{\substack{\text{error} \\ \text{variance}}} \quad (3)$$

The sum of the common variances can be represented by an additional symbol (h_j^2):

$$a_{j1}^2 + a_{j2}^2 + \ldots + a_{jr}^2 = h_j^2 \quad (4)$$

and, thus, the total variance can be expressed as:

$$h_j^2 + s_j^2 + e_j^2 = 1.0 \quad (5)$$

In these terms, reliable variance can be expressed as:[14]

$$r_{jj} = h_j^2 + s_j^2 = 1 - e_j^2 \quad (6)$$

and unique variance as:

$$u_j^2 = s_j^2 + e_j^2 = 1 - h_j^2 \quad (7)$$

Or, to summarize these five variances, the bar in Figure VII-4 can be used:

Figure VII-4

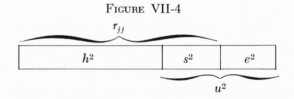

Given a correlation matrix permeated by the types of variance defined above, the process of factor analysis transforms this matrix into a factor matrix that presents the pattern of common variance, as in Figure VII-5.

FIGURE VII-5

FACTORS

		1	2	3	. . .	P
V	1	a_{11}	a_{12}	a_{13}	. . .	a_{1p}
A	2	a_{21}	a_{22}	a_{23}	. . .	a_{2p}
R						
I	3	a_{31}	a_{32}	a_{33}	. . .	a_{3p}
A	.	.	.	.		.
B						
L	.	.	.	.		.
E						
S	.	.	.	.		.
	M	a_{n1}	a_{n2}	a_{n3}	. . .	a_{np}

Each column of this matrix represents a factor, and each row represents a variable. The number of columns (factors) is almost always fewer than the number of rows (variables), since an essential aim of factor analysis is to reduce the factorial complexity of the correlation matrix to a number smaller than the number of variables.

The elements within the factor matrix are called *factor loadings*. If, for the sake of exposition, we concentrate on the simpler case, in which the factors are uncorrelated or *orthogonal* (i.e., have themselves no shared variance), these loadings are equal to the correlations of the variables with the factors.[15] For example, a_{11} represents the correlation between variable 1 and factor 1: Thus, squaring a_{11} would tell us how much variance variable 1 shares with factor 1.

Knowing the relationship of the factor loadings to the variables, we might ask what relationship these loadings have to the original *correlations* among variables. This relationship is defined in factor theory to be the following: *The correlation between any two variables is the sum of the cross-products of their loadings on a set of orthogonal, common factors.* This is expressed, using the first two variables in Figure VII-5, in the following equation:

$$r_{12} = a_{11}\, a_{21} + a_{12}\, a_{22} + a_{13}\, a_{23} + \ldots + a_{1n}\, a_{2n} \qquad (8)$$

where a_{11} = loading of factor 1 on variable 1, and

a_{21} = loading of factor 1 on variable 2, etc.

We can illustrate this relationship concretely by examining a hypothetical factor matrix with the common, specific, reliable, and error variance added and only three variables actually given numerical values (Table VII-1). Specific variance, reliable variance, and error variance ordinarily are not obtained in an actual factor analysis. They are presented here for illustrative purposes.

TABLE VII-1

HYPOTHETICAL FACTOR MATRIX

	Factor						
Variable	A	B	C	h^2	s^2	r_{jj}	e^2
1	.7	.4	.0	.65	.12	.77	.23
2	.4	.2	.8	.84	.10	.94	.06
3	.2	.7	.5	.78	.07	.85	.15
.							
.							
.							
M							

These variables also can be represented in terms of variance by the bar diagrams in Figure VII-6.

Using these hypothetical values and equation (8), the correlation between variables 1 and 2 can be computed as follows:

$$r_{12} = (.7)_{11} \, (.4)_{21} + (.4)_{12} \, (.2)_{22} + (.0)_{13} \, (.8)_{23} = .36$$
$$\quad\;\; .28 \qquad\qquad .08 \qquad\qquad .00$$

This correlation is composed largely of the common loadings on factor A (.28). Similarly,

$$r_{13} = (.7)_{11} \, (.2)_{31} + (.4)_{12} \, (.7)_{32} + (.0)_{13} \, (.5)_{33} = .42$$
$$\quad\;\; .14 \qquad\qquad .28 \qquad\qquad .00$$

and

$$r_{23} = (.4)_{21} \, (.2)_{31} + (.2)_{22} \, (.7)_{32} + (.8)_{23} \, (.5)_{33} = .62$$
$$\quad\;\; .08 \qquad\qquad .14 \qquad\qquad .40$$

FIGURE VII-6

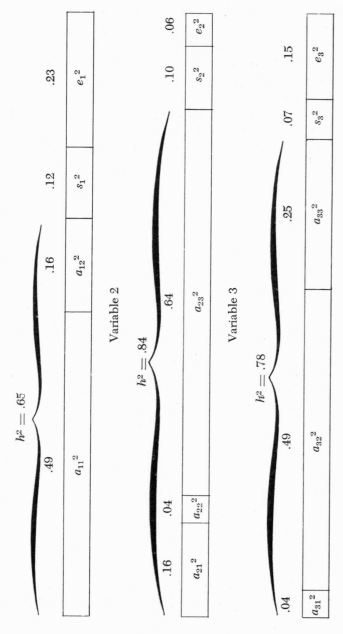

Variable 1

Variable 2

Variable 3

Here, factors B (.28) and C (.40) are, respectively, the most important.

THE GEOMETRICAL INTERPRETATION OF FACTORS[16]

Relationships between correlations, factor loadings, and the types of variance can also be illustrated geometrically, a procedure that may facilitate understanding of factor theory.[17] Figure VII-7 presents a common-factor space of the first two factors, A and B, and the first two variables, 1 and 2, of Table VII-1.

FIGURE VII-7

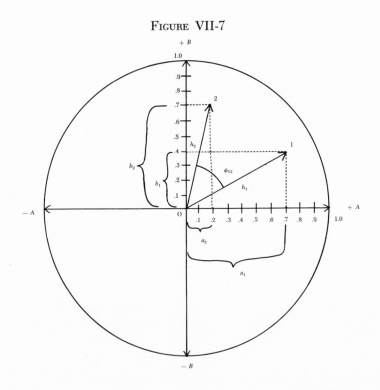

Factor A is represented by the horizontal axis; Factor B, by the vertical axis. Factors represented by axes perpendicular to each other are orthogonal (independent) in that their moving along either axis, or any line parallel to either axis, causes no change in the value of the other axis.

The circle in Figure VII-7 has a radius of unity. Both factors *A* and *B* and variables 1 and 2 are represented by vectors (lines having given lengths and given directions). The factor vectors are of unit length because all their variance is common variance. The variable vectors, on the other hand, are less than unit length because they also have unique variance, which, if represented in a geometric space, would require an additional dimension for each variable.

In a common-factor space, there are as many dimensions as there are common factors. A third orthogonal factor would be placed through the origin at right angles to the first two. Additional factors can be added indefinitely, if only in one's imagination, at right angles to all preceding factors.[18]

Returning to Figure VII-7, we note that dotted lines have been drawn from the ends of the variable vectors perpendicular to the two reference axes—variable 1 has a projection of a_1 on axis *A* and a projection of b_1 on axis *B*, etc. These distances from the origin to the points at which the perpendiculars cut the axes are the coordinates of the variable vectors. Thus, the coordinates of variable vector 1 are (.7, .4), and the coordinates of variable vector 2 are (.2, .7). These coordinates represent the factor loadings of variables 1 and 2 on factors *A* and *B*, as can be seen by referring back to Table VII-1. We have already seen that squaring the factor loadings of a variable gives the communality of that variable. Thus, in our geometric illustration, the communality of variable 1 is equal to $a_1^2 + b_1^2$ and analagously for variable 2 (ignoring for the moment the third factor). Note also that a_1 and b_1 are the legs of a right triangle whose hypotenuse is the vector for variable 1. Since h^2 is the square of the hypotenuse (from the Pythagorean theorem), it follows that the length of the variable vector equals h, the square root of the communality.

We can now define the intercorrelations of variables geometrically, using h as previously defined in an equation derived by Thurstone:[19]

$$r_{ij} = h_i h_j \cos \phi_{ij} \qquad\qquad (9)$$

where r_{ij} = correlation between variables I and J,
  $h_i h_j$ = lengths of vectors for variables I and J, respectively, and
  ϕ_{ij} = angle of separation between vectors I and J.

That is, the correlation between two variables is equal to the product of the lengths of their vectors times the cosine of their angle of separation. The cosine of an angle varies between 1.0 and 0.0 as the angle varies between 0 and 90 degrees respectively. We can see from equation (9) that if both variable vectors (h's) equal unity (which they rarely do in a common-factor space), the correlation is determined entirely by $\cos \phi_{ij}$. Under these conditions, if the vectors have an angle of 0 degrees (i.e., are colinear), the correlation is +1.0. If they are separated by 90 degrees, the correlation is 0.[20] When the vectors are separated by more than 90 degrees, they correlate negatively and approach a correlation of −1.0 as their separation approaches 180 degrees and their lengths approach unity. These relationships are illustrated in Figures VII-8 and VII-9.

FIGURE VII-8

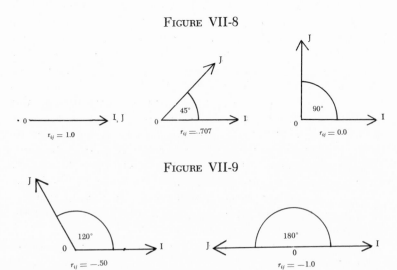

FIGURE VII-9

The fact that correlations can be represented by vectors and angles is relevant to the determination of the number of factors or dimensions in a correlation matrix. Assuming vectors of unit length for the sake of simplicity, we can use the correlations derived from Table VII-1 for illustrative purposes. The angular separation between these correlations is presented in Figure VII-10, where, for example, a correlation of .36 equals the cosine of a 69-degree angle.

FIGURE VII-10

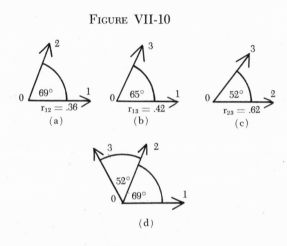

As can be seen in Figure VII-10 (d), the correlations between variables 1 and 2 and between variables 2 and 3 can accurately be represented in two-dimensional space. However, the sum of their angles (121°) does not equal the angle required (65°) for correct representation of the correlation between variables 1 and 3. This means that a two-dimensional space does not portray adequately the relationships among these variables; at least three factors are needed.[21]

We can now see that different correlation matrices will require varying numbers of dimensions to be accurately represented in an *n*-dimensional space. In fact,

> *what factor analysis means by factors is . . . nothing more than the dimensions (independent coordinate axes) of the space required to contain a certain set of correlations when they are spatially represented.*[22]

FACTOR EXTRACTION

Given the task just indicated, several methods for obtaining a factor solution have been devised. Perhaps the most commonly used of these is the principal-axes (or principal-components) method. The distinguishing characteristic of this method is that in it each factor extracts the maximum amount of variance (i.e., the sum of squares of the factor loadings), leaving the smallest possible residual variance. This procedure condenses the correlation matrix into the smallest possible number of orthogonal factors. It is impossible within the scope of this book to detail the computational procedures involved in this or in other methods. Fortunately, electronic computers have come to the aid of the factor analyst. Information on some of the computer programs available for this work is presented in Chapter VIII.[23] At this juncture, a few general comments are in order.

A major decision confronting the factor analyst concerns the values to be placed in the principal diagonal of the correlation matrix before beginning the factor analysis. Since variables correlate perfectly with themselves, the diagonal would ordinarily be filled with 1.0's. If these values are retained, the factor analysis is based on the total variance within the correlation matrix. It is also possible to base the analysis on reliable variance or, more commonly, on common variance. In the latter cases, the values are rarely known in advance and must be estimated. Fortunately, such estimates may be slightly inaccurate without seriously distorting the factor structure.[24] In estimating common variance, one possible procedure is to use, for each variable, the highest correlation of that variable with the other correlations in the matrix. Another is to use, for each variable, its squared multiple correlation with all other variables. When total or reliable variance is factored, specific or error factors may be extracted in addition to common factors. As their nomenclature indicates, these factors are composed of specific and error variance, respectively. A specific factor will have a high loading on only one variable, whereas an error factor will have *no* high loadings. The type of variance and the mode of estimation used in a particular factor analysis depend on the preferences and purposes of the investigator. The issues such decisions involve are complex, and the reader is referred to more specialized material.[25]

The researcher must decide also the type of correlation coefficient that is to be used in constructing the correlation matrix. When the variables are continuous, the Pearson r (product moment) is considered the most satisfactory. Controversy exists concerning which coefficients are most appropriate when the variables are discrete. This issue is particularly relevant to roll-call analysis, in which responses are coded in discrete, polytomous categories. In the case of dichotomies, phi (ϕ), phi over maximum phi ($\phi/\phi\text{max}$), and tetrachoric r are most often used.[26] Phi, the product-moment coefficient for the dichotomous case, is generally adequate. When responses are coded in more than two categories, other procedures may be used. For example, in the illustration presented later in this chapter, responses are trichotomized and coded $yea = 1$, $nay = -1$, and $no\ response = 0$, with a product moment coefficient resulting.[27] Again, the reader may wish to consult specialized writings.

FACTOR ROTATION

As we noted earlier, the correlations among variables determine a geometric configuration of variable vectors in an n-dimensional hypersphere. This configuration is invariant—that is, no other configuration is possible for a given correlation matrix. It is important to realize, however, that the reference axes or vectors (i.e., factor vectors) are essentially arbitrary; an infinite number of combinations of these axes could be used to represent a given correlation matrix. This, of course, means that the factor loadings appearing in the factor matrix are arbitrary. The loadings derived in a factor analysis result from the mathematical manipulations involved in the particular method used. One implication of this fact is that the reference axes can be *rotated* around the origin anywhere in the hypersphere, and the factor loadings of the variables can be recalculated in reference to their new locations. Because investigators usually want factors with clear significance that can be compared with factors in other studies, rotation is often used as a second stage in factor analysis.[28] The

location of the reference vectors must therefore rest upon interpretations of the data and upon theoretical and conceptual
considerations.

One common principle used for rotation is that of *simple
structure*, proposed by Thurstone.[29] Its aim is to establish a
relatively standard location for the reference axes, a location
that minimizes the factorial complexity of the variables. The
criteria for a simple structure are the following:

1. Each variable should have at least one loading close to zero.

2. For each factor column, there should be at least as many
   variables with zero loadings as there are factors.

3. For every pair of factors, there should be several variables
   loaded on one factor but not on the other.

4. For solutions having four or more factors, a large proportion of the variables should have loadings close to zero on
   any pair of factors.

5. Only a small number of variables should have appreciable
   loadings on any given pair of factors.

These criteria are illustrated in Table VII-2, in which the *X*'s
stand for appreciable loadings.

TABLE VII-2

Factor

Variable	I	II	III
1	X		
2		X	
3			X
4	X	X	
5	X	X	
6	X		X
7	X		X
8		X	X
9		X	X
10		X	X

Thurstone's criteria have no absolute validity and must be related to the investigator's problems. Other criteria may be more useful in certain situations—rotation to agree with past findings, rotation to agree with factors from past factor analyses, and the like.[30]

Aside from the criteria to be used, the major decision to be made before rotation is whether to rotate orthogonally or obliquely—another controversial topic among factor analysts. Those who favor orthogonal rotation use the following arguments: (1) The independent factors obtained in orthogonal rotation are theoretically preferable; (2) such rotation is simpler to work with, both computationally and graphically; (3) the obliqueness of axes is subject to sampling instability; and (4) little difference in the interpretation of the results is found no matter which method is used. Advocates of oblique rotation counter as follows: (1) The amount of obliqueness is important and should be taken into account in interpretation; (2) simple structure is more adequately obtained from use of oblique rotation; and (3) obliqueness reflects a more valid picture of nature, in which variables are often related.[31]

THE NATURE OF FACTORS

Up to this point we have defined and treated factors as mathematical and statistical concepts. Some social scientists go no further. Others prefer to give these statistical "outcomes" further theoretical meaning.[32] Psychologists, for example, often speak of factors as representing "functional unities." For those who adhere to the statistical interpretation, this means, simply, that a factor represents a reproducible pattern of variance shared by variables. For the more theoretical in outlook, the idea of functional unity may signify a number of different kinds of interrelationships.[33] It may refer to a high level of causal interaction among the variables, as in Figure VII-11(a). In these terms, factors represent clusters of causally related variables.

A factor may represent also a common source or cause of the individual variables, which themselves are not causally related. (See Figure VII-11(b).)[34] In more complex fashion, the ob-

FIGURE VII-11

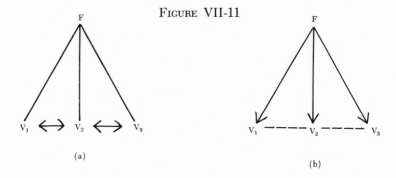

(a)

(b)

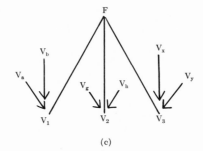

(c)

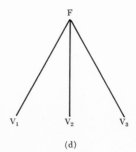

(d)

——>   Indicates a causal relationship. The direction of the arrow shows the flow of causality.

– – – –   Indicates that there is a high correlation between variables but no causal relationship.

————   Indicates that a factor *represents* the statistical interrelationships among variables but does not *cause* these interrelationships.

served variables may be separately caused by a number of other variables, the high correlations among them being essentially spurious. (See Figure VII-11 (c).) A fourth interpretation would equate a factor with a concept and would treat variables loading highly on that factor as indicators of that concept. (See Figure VII-11(d).) This last approach refers in a general way to the idea of *operationalizing* concepts.[35] In this conception, the variables we observe are often only imperfect representations of the more abstract concepts with which we are dealing.[36] Observed variables are thus only operational *approximations*. Percentage of the population living in cities of more than 20,000 (urban population) may, for example, be an imperfect representation of what one means by *urbanization*. Population per square mile (population density) may tap another aspect of this general concept. Factor analysis is available as a method of index construction in which the various imperfect indicators of a concept are weighted according to their factor loadings or some other appropriate criterion.

Finally, a factor may represent a *combination* of these patterns of relationships. In roll-call analysis, an investigator may have in mind any of these "models," or any combination of them, before, during, and after the analysis. It is probably the case, however, that Figure VII-11(b) generally approximates the ideas of the roll-call analyst. For example, the main thrust of Turner's *Party and Constituency*[37] is that the two factors designated in the title of his book are the major underlying causes of the clustering of roll-call votes and of legislators.

INTERPRETATION OF FACTORS

When he has obtained rotated factor loadings, the investigator is faced with the problem of interpreting his results. On the theoretical level, he must rely on his conception of the nature of the factors and his familiarity with his subject matter. On the practical level, the usual procedure is to base the interpretation on common attributes of the variables with high loadings on a factor that are detectable to a lesser degree in variables with moderate loadings and absent in variables with low loadings.[38]

Interpretation may be facilitated also by computation of *factor scores*. The general goal in computing factor scores is to find a weighted combination of the variables that best predict a factor. The general formula is:

$$X_f = \sum_{i=1}^{p} \beta_i X_i$$

where X_f = the factor score,

β_i = the weighting coefficient for the ith variable,

X_i = the raw score for the individual on the ith variable, and

p = the number of variables that load on the factor.

The weighting coefficients (β_i's) are the regression weights obtained through a multiple correlation using the factor as the criterion variable and the original variables as the predictors. The determination of p is left to the investigator. It is possible to use *all* the variables for each factor score, but typically only those loading highest on the factor are used.[39]

When this process is completed, each unit will have a factor score for each factor retained in the analysis. By examining the distribution of factor scores for a given factor, one can identify those units that contribute most highly to the factor loadings. Knowledge of what these units hold in common that differentiate them from units with low factor scores may lead to further development or modification of the interpretation of the factor. In a factor analysis of U.S. Senate roll calls, for example, examination of the factor scores of senators on one of the factors might suggest a regional interpretation if all senators from Southern states are clustered at one end of the factor score distribution.

In addition to contributing to interpretation of the relationships among roll calls, computation of factor scores provides a method alternative to bloc analysis for deriving clusters or blocs of units. This clustering of units can be examined *directly* by what is called *Q*-technique factor analysis, the transpose of the usual R-technique.[40] Returning to the basic data matrix of Figure VII-1, we recall that we constructed the correlation matrix from this matrix by correlating each pair of variables (columns) over the values of the N units. To construct a correlation matrix for Q-technique factor analysis, we correlate each pair of units (rows) across the values of the M variables. The resulting correlation matrix would be identical to the one presented in Figure VII-2, except that *Units* would replace *Variables* at the top and side of the matrix (and N would replace M). And, of course, the factor matrix derived from this set of Q correlations would have units rather than variables occupying the rows.[41] The analysis proceeds as before, except that the interpretation rests on detecting *common traits among the units* that load highly on a given factor, rather than among the variables. One could, of course, compute factor scores and examine the clustering of variables, thus completing the transposition of techniques.[42]

Recalling the factor analytic studies briefly mentioned in the introductory section of this chapter, we can now note that a major difference in their procedures results from the fact that Carlson and Harrell, Harris, and Grumm all used Q-technique, whereas Alker used R-technique. In this way, the former authors directly obtained clusters of legislators, but Alker directly obtained clusters of variables. By computing factor scores, Alker was able also to derive clusters of nations and to examine the positions of these nations on the factors.

AN ILLUSTRATION OF FACTOR ANALYSIS

To make this discussion more concrete, we shall attempt to work through the major steps of a factor analysis of legislative voting in the 1961 Senate. The analysis will proceed from the selection of the sample of roll calls used to the factor analysis itself, which will consist of (1) the derivation of a matrix of correlations among roll-call votes; (2) the extraction of factors and the presentation of a factor matrix; (3) the rotation of factors to a "simplified" solution; and (4) the investigation of individual legislators' positions on the factors. The analysis will be carried out using the MESA I computer program (described more fully in Chaper VIII), which derives orthogonal factors according to the principal-axes method of factor analysis.

The R-technique of factor analysis was chosen for this design because it will enable us to investigate the interrelationships *among roll-call votes* during the particular session selected for study. The result will, we hope, be a matrix of common factors that "underlie" the set of bills chosen for analysis. If it is true that the large number of more or less discrete issues in a legislative session can be reduced to a relatively small number of "dimensions," then R-analysis should perform the task for us. To make further use of the statistical design in examining the positions of individuals on the dimensions, we shall derive a score on each factor for each senator. The distribution of these scores will enable us to place legislators into groups and to explicate further the nature of the factor structure.

THE SELECTING OF A SAMPLE OF ROLL CALLS
TO BE FACTOR-ANALYZED

As we suggested in Chapter V, the selection of an appropriate sample of roll calls is an important first step in conducting any study of legislative voting. Because the criteria for selection may color or bias the findings of the analysis, it is usually desirable to discuss explicitly the particular criteria employed.

In our analysis, it was decided that the sample should include only issues of high conflict in the legislature, i.e., those involving participation of a large number of legislators and a close division of the vote. Since these dual criteria are included in the coefficient of significance presented by William Riker, his computational method was used (see Chapter V). Using the VOTES program written for the CDC 3400 computer, a coefficient of significance was calculated for each of 204 roll calls taken in the 1961 United States Senate, and the resulting values were ranked in descending order of significance. Table VII-3 illustrates the output obtained by this method and presents the upper portion of the sample as ordered by the program.

TABLE VII-3
RANKING OF THE FIFTY MOST SIGNIFICANT ROLL CALLS IN THE
1961 SESSION OF THE UNITED STATES SENATE
(ACCORDING TO THE RIKER COEFFICIENT OF SIGNIFICANCE)

RANK	BILL ID	COEFFICIENT OF SIGNIFICANCE
1	1	0.9323
2	30	0.9192
3	131	0.9056
4	141	0.9053
5	5	0.9050
6	134	0.9045
7	135	0.8920
8	136	0.8914
9	72	0.8912
10	65	0.8784
11	137	0.8784
12	62	0.8781
13	71	0.8776
14	66	0.8640
15	57	0.8509
16	27	0.8391
17	61	0.8389
18	98	0.8389
19	162	0.8373
20	177	0.8370
21	146	0.8368
22	29	0.8253
23	130	0.8253
24	28	0.8250
25	100	0.8247
26	59	0.8242
27	74	0.8237
28	84	0.8237
29	90	0.8237
30	163	0.8237
31	70	0.8234
32	69	0.8234
33	152	0.8232
34	121	0.8111
35	154	0.8111
36	150	0.8109
37	91	0.8109
38	123	0.8109
39	164	0.8106
40	67	0.8101
41	16	0.8098
42	14	0.8096
43	133	0.7986
44	138	0.7983
45	122	0.7983
46	77	0.7981
47	64	0.7981
48	45	0.7973
49	94	0.7960
50	26	0.7858

Although the initial inclination was to select the top twenty-five issues in the sample of roll calls, the twenty-five "most significant" votes were found to represent only nine discrete bills. The extensive duplication apparently resulted from successive votes on amendments to the same bill; coefficients of significance on related amendments were usually similar because the voting alignments were fairly consistent. Therefore, all duplicated issues were eliminated, so that only the roll call with the highest coefficient was included from a particular set of related motions. In order to obtain a sample size of 25, successive roll calls were considered until the appropriate number of discrete bills were reached. In all, the top ranking 86 from a total of 204 roll calls had to be considered before enough votes were selected. Table VII-4 describes each of the roll calls in the sample. Note that the ranking on the left corresponds to the number of each roll call within the sample analyzed; the second number represents the designation given the roll call by the *Congressional Quarterly*, from which the data were originally obtained.[43] The six-letter code following each description indicates the name of the variable as it appears in the correlation matrix and factor matrices.

TABLE VII-4
IDENTIFICATION OF ROLL CALLS SELECTED FOR ANALYSIS

Number	CQ Number	Coefficient of Significance	Description
1	1	.9323	Proposal to revise Rule 22 to enable 3/5 rather than 2/3 of Senators to invoke cloture. Dirksen motion to refer to committee. (RULE 22)
2	5	.9050	Amendment to Area Redevelopment Act. Yea supports President's position. (ARA)
3	16	.8098	Amendment to Temporary Extended Unemployment Compensation Act. Nay supports President's position. (UNEMPL)
4	23	.7170	Amendment relating to the Sugar Act of 1948 and the Dominican

			quota (regarding the Cuban cutback). Yea supports President's position. (SUGAR)
5	30	.9192	Amendment to Fair Labor Standards Act. Nay supports President's position. (LABSTN)
6	45	.7973	Amendment to include maintenance costs in School Assistance Act. (SCHOOL)
7	57	.8509	Amendment to add to the Appropriations for Department of the Interior. Yea supports President's position. (INTDEP)
8	72	.8912	Amendment to Housing Act. Yea supports President's position. (HOUSING)
9	77	.7981	Amendment relating to Federal Aid to Highways. Nay supports President's position. ($-HWAY)
10	79	.7839	Resolution disapproving President's reorganization plan for Securities and Exchange Commission. Nay supports President's position. (REORG)
11	90	.8237	Amendment to Educational and Cultural Exchange Act. (E-CEX)
12	98	.8389	Amendment to Agricultural Act designed to cut the right of cooperatives to join federations. Nay supports President's position. (AGRACT)
13	113	.7832	Proxmire amendment to cut radiology defense funds. Yea supports President's position. ($-IND)
14	121	.8111	Appropriations for Departments of Labor and Health, Education, and Welfare. Yea supports President's position. ($-HEW)
15	125	.7290	Mundt motion to suspend rules on Defense appropriations and offer amendment to the extension of federal aid to impacted school areas.

			Nay supports President's position. ($-DEF)
16	131	.9056	Dirksen amendment to require the President to submit to Congressional approval foreign assistance loans exceeding $5 million. (FORAST)
17	152	.8232	Amendment to Manpower Training Act. Nay supports President's position. (MANPOW)
18	156	.7042	Amendment to reduce Peace Corps authorization. Nay supports President's position. ($-PEACE)
19	157	.7154	Motion relating to Major G. H. Williams promotion to Brigadier General in U.S. Army Reserves. Nay supports President's position. (MAJORS)
20	161	.8373	Mansfield motion relating to Civil Rights Commission. (CIVRTS)
21	170	.7416	Amendment relating to financing of federally subsidized vessels under the 1936 Merchant Marine Act. (MERCH)
22	176	.7439	Tower amendment relating to the Small Business Act. (SBA)
23	177	.8370	Goldwater amendment relating to the establishment of Arms Control and Disarmament Agency for World Peace. Nay supports President's position. (ARMCON)
24	182	.7688	Amendment to extend Mexican Farm Labor program (Mansfield motion). (MEXLAB)
25	185	.7693	Morse amendment to extend laws of Federal Aid to Impacted School Districts. Yea supports President's position. ($-SCHL)

Range of significance coefficients in sample = .7042 — .9323.

Parenthesized symbols of six letters or less are variable names that identify the roll calls used in the analysis. The matrices of correlations and factors make use of these symbols to simplify presentation.

It may be argued that this selection procedure gives undue weight to those roll calls that seem significant but are not repeated several times, as were amendments to housing or foreign assistance in that session. This is true in the sense that only one foreign assistance amendment and one housing amendment were included in the final sample used in the analysis. However, the rationale for the method was not to obtain a random sample representing a cross-section of the legislature's activities, but to maximize the substantive content of the factors while not "swamping" the analysis with too many duplicated measures. In any factor analysis, procedures are dictated by the needs of the project, the needs of the researcher, and the resources available to the project—there is no single prescription for the selection of the sample.

THE CORRELATION MATRIX

Our data include the responses of 101 Senators to 25 selected roll-call votes taken in the 1961 session of the United States Senate. (Naturally, only 100 were eligible to vote at one time, but the replacement of Blakley (D-Texas) by Tower (R-Texas) in mid-session increased the total sample to be considered for that session.) For our purposes, it seemed useful to eliminate paired responses and announced votes and to consider only the *effective* division of "yeas" and "nays": that is, the responses of those *present and voting* at the roll-call stage. After the example of Carl McMurray's experimentation with factorial methods,[44] the responses were coded as follows: 1 = yea; −1 = nay; 0 = no vote.

Alternative strategies for coding responses exist, and the method chosen will have some consequence for the factor structure derived.[45] The choice in this case may be defended on two grounds. The first is that the numerical values have some intuitive justification based on the positive and negative signs given "yeas" and "nays." The zero value for a "no vote" simply means that no position was taken at the voting stage. The second favorable characteristic of this coding scheme is that the values assigned are compatible with most computer routines for factor analysis. The correlation coefficient generated is a Pearson product-moment statistic.

The major alternative to the method used is that of coding responses as one ("yea") and zero ("nay"). This procedure produces a matrix of phi-coefficients when the correlations are computed. (For a discussion of the phi-coefficient, see Chapter III.) The theoretical position of the researcher in using the phi, or the related phi/phi-max, is that the items (roll calls) are essentially dichotomous and that missing responses need not be considered. Depending upon whether one accepts this position, either coding procedure is acceptable—as long as the researcher is aware of the relationship between the numerical coding and the correlation coefficient used.[46]

When the data of our example had been selected and recoded according to the criteria we have discussed, they were processed at the Northwestern University Computing Center with IBM 709 and CDC 3400 computers. The factor analysis with rotation was performed by the MESA I computer routine. Several examples of the output of this routine appear later in this chapter to illustrate the stages of a factorial solution. The correlation matrix, representing the relationships between roll calls, is reproduced with slight modification in Table VII-5.

Notice that the correlation matrix contains only the values that fall in and below the diagonal. It does so because the upper right-hand portion of the matrix duplicates the coefficients in the left-hand section. The coefficients in the diagonal have values of unity because the variable correlates perfectly with itself.

When correlations are presented in this form, one can give substantial interpretation to the matrix as it exists, much as the Q matrix in Chapter VI was interpreted. One can, for example, scan the matrix by rows or columns to determine which roll-call votes relate closely to any one bill. By considering one bill at a time, one can gain some information about its relation to the issues involved in other motions on which the legislature voted during the same session. It is interesting but not surprising to note, for example, that the vote on Rule 22, Senate cloture (variable 1), is related to voting on the Civil Rights Commission (variable 20). If the correlations by pair that each of the variables has with other variables in the matrix are traced, one can gain an approximation of a simple "factor analysis" by inspecting the pattern of correlations. Clearly, though, the number of variables that a researcher can keep in mind at a single time is limited, and it is virtually impossible to follow the pattern of interrelationships in even a medium-sized matrix, such as this one. After all, the number of individual coefficients is equal to $n(n-1)/2$ (where $n =$ the number of variables) or, in this case, 300.

THE UNROTATED FACTOR MATRIX

To cope with the difficulty of summarizing the patterns in a matrix of correlations, we need a procedure for expressing meaningfully the common characteristics of a set of roll calls. Factor analysis will do this by "simplifying" the set of relationships and expressing them as a set of "factors," which actually are statistical representations of the patterns existing in the correlation matrix. Table VII-6 illustrates the first approximation of factor analysis to this simplification of underlying relationships, the unrotated factor matrix.

A few remarks about the table may help in the interpretation of the factor matrix. Variables are listed vertically by their abbreviated name designations (see Table VII-4 for full identification) along the left side, and communalities (h^2) appear directly to their right. The communalities listed apply to the first ten unrotated factors, all of which are reproduced in this table. Together, the ten factors account for 83.2% of the variance in the original matrix. The first factor accounts for the largest single proportion of variance, and the succeeding factors account for decreasing amounts. The decrease in variance is characteristic of the statistical method, which extracts the largest proportion of common variance for the first factor and increasingly smaller proportions for each succeeding factor. Each factor is extracted from residual variance not accounted for by earlier factors.

Another feature of Table VII-6 is the designation *sum squares,* computationally the sum of the squared factor loadings, which is

TABLE VII-5

CORRELATION MATRIX FOR 25 ROLL CALLS IN THE 1961 SENATE*

ROLL CALL	1	2	3	4	5	6	7	8	9	10	11
1. RULE 22	100										
2. ARA	40	100									
3. UNEMPL	23	74	100								
4. SUGAR	−02	43	−10	100							
5. LABSTN	62	−60	48	−08	100						
6. SCHOOL	08	−42	−44	−06	−15	100					
7. INTDEP	−18	−75	−66	−04	−42	49	100				
8. HOUSING	−45	−77	−65	02	−73	27	59	100			
9. $-HWAY	48	31	12	05	45	06	−12	−32	100		
10. REORG	14	62	62	−08	37	−42	−59	−49	−02	100	
11. E-CEX	28	75	67	−08	52	−49	−66	−60	22	59	100
12. AGRACT	−11	00	11	−18	03	−34	−13	−05	−16	07	12
13. $-IND	−03	16	34	−44	09	−23	−18	−19	−20	23	18
14. $-HEW	15	63	62	−08	38	−57	−69	−50	04	59	61
15. $-DEF	24	82	68	05	51	−48	−66	−67	18	65	71
16. FORAST	−39	−54	−48	09	−47	18	42	50	−20	−37	−49
17. MANPOW	25	83	67	10	56	−41	−68	−73	21	65	71
18. $-PEACE	29	64	57	−03	55	−45	−66	−58	14	56	64
19. MAJORS	−10	43	57	−06	20	−54	−52	−33	−12	56	51
20. CIVRTS	72	37	24	09	56	07	−16	−40	42	11	20
21. MERCH	08	33	36	−23	19	−18	−29	−29	05	30	28
22. SBA	15	49	42	−07	38	−35	−50	−48	03	48	45
23. ARMCON	26	70	52	03	48	−28	−57	−60	30	46	55
24. MEXLAB	−50	−58	−41	00	−61	12	44	62	−40	−39	−55
25. $-SCHL	−48	−36	−52	02	−65	23	55	67	−38	−43	−57

TABLE VII-5
(continued)

12	13	14	15	16	17	18	19	20	21	22	23	24	25
100													
35	100												
28	43	100											
06	24	63	100										
−02	−24	−38	−46	100									
07	20	65	85	−57	100								
24	26	61	70	−40	72	100							
33	24	53	50	−15	47	54	100						
−07	−11	11	27	−36	28	28	−03	100					
14	21	29	37	−20	32	29	18	08	100				
25	22	47	55	−35	52	69	38	15	27	100			
13	10	48	64	−45	66	63	28	34	−22	42	100		
03	−05	−37	−54	41	−55	−51	−21	−34	−26	−42	−55	100	
01	02	−36	−52	44	−64	−63	−30	−48	−22	−47	−64	62	100

*All correlations have been multiplied by 100 and rounded off to the second decimal place.

the amount of variance the factor shares with the 25 variables (see the discussion above on page 129). The sum of squares may be represented by the formula,

$$SS = \sum_{i=1}^{m} a_i^2$$

where SS is the sum of squares of the variable loadings on a
factor,
m is the number of variables, and
a_i is the loading of the ith variable on the factor.

TABLE VII-6

R-FACTOR ANALYSIS OF 1961 SENATE ROLL CALL VOTES.

SAMPLE SELECTED WITH RIKER COEFFICIENT OF SIGNIFICANCE.

UNROTATED FACTOR MATRIX

			1	2	3
SUM SQUARES	FACTOR NUMBER		10.798	3.130	1.556
VARIABLE NO.	NAME	COMMUNALITY 10 FACTORS			
1	RULE22	0.856	-0.422	0.666	-0.293
2	ARA	0.880	-0.905	0.087	0.116
3	UNEMPL	0.795	-0.797	-0.172	-0.030
4	SUGAR	0.952	0.035	0.239	0.773
5	LABSTN	0.823	-0.705	0.434	-0.118
6	SCHOOL	0.815	0.503	0.500	-0.229
7	INTDEP	0.710	0.793	0.184	-0.184
8	HOUSNG	0.797	0.820	-0.199	0.062
9	$-HWAY	0.838	-0.290	0.636	-0.042
10	REORG	0.725	-0.713	-0.266	0.102
11	E-CEX	0.770	-0.817	-0.087	0.067
12	AGRACT	0.887	-0.157	-0.476	-0.322
13	$-IND	0.881	-0.272	-0.481	-0.608
14	$-HEW	0.759	-0.737	-0.360	-0.026
15	$-DEF	0.808	-0.868	-0.083	0.145
16	FORAST	0.852	0.611	-0.169	0.226
17	MANPOW	0.850	-0.881	-0.026	0.159
18	$PEACE	0.807	-0.821	-0.120	0.015
19	MAJORS	0.812	-0.555	-0.517	0.165
20	CIVRTS	0.880	-0.403	0.641	-0.172
21	MERCH	0.986	-0.393	-0.156	-0.312
22	SBA	0.883	-0.641	-0.179	-0.049
23	ARMCON	0.858	-0.742	0.118	0.078
24	MEXLAB	0.763	0.677	-0.327	0.048
25	$-SCHL	0.806	0.768	-0.322	-0.038

The maximum amount of variance a factor can share with a set of variables is the sum of perfect correlations (factor loadings of 1.0) with all m variables. If we thus divide the preceding formula by m, we obtain

$$\frac{SS}{m} = \frac{\sum\limits_{i=1}^{m} a_i^2}{m}$$, the *proportion* of total variance.

This particular figure is of importance to the factor analysis carried out here because it indicates the total percentage of variance

Table VII-6

(continued)

4	5	6	7	8	9	10
1.068	0.879	0.782	0.735	0.704	0.585	0.556
0.169	-0.195	-0.050	-0.159	-0.178	0.042	0.142
-0.146	-0.061	-0.057	0.002	0.050	-0.060	-0.073
-0.181	-0.197	-0.123	-0.066	-0.103	-0.016	-0.164
0.234	-0.095	0.083	-0.316	0.278	0.210	-0.068
0.178	-0.063	0.005	-0.052	-0.042	0.277	-0.079
-0.243	0.139	0.292	0.031	-0.085	0.033	-0.295
0.040	0.031	0.063	-0.020	-0.020	0.054	-0.050
0.043	0.016	-0.036	-0.013	-0.030	-0.186	0.206
0.069	0.080	-0.454	0.296	0.134	0.065	0.148
-0.212	-0.060	0.089	-0.075	-0.267	0.009	0.038
-0.079	-0.063	-0.157	0.163	-0.045	-0.043	0.156
0.658	0.128	-0.109	-0.020	0.172	-0.121	-0.159
-0.027	-0.271	0.118	0.054	0.179	0.260	-0.124
0.054	-0.188	-0.091	-0.009	0.109	0.137	0.090
-0.124	0.034	0.033	-0.048	0.058	0.005	-0.053
0.146	0.299	-0.265	0.038	-0.283	0.259	-0.264
-0.116	-0.025	0.100	-0.025	0.139	-0.008	-0.065
0.225	0.171	0.167	0.017	-0.084	-0.014	0.063
0.137	-0.055	-0.147	0.016	-0.387	-0.011	-0.130
0.258	-0.167	-0.012	-0.330	-0.157	-0.211	-0.067
-0.330	0.473	-0.303	-0.514	0.145	-0.003	0.027
0.208	0.361	0.400	-0.038	-0.090	0.086	0.295
0.036	0.143	0.072	0.193	0.262	-0.301	-0.252
0.043	-0.261	-0.039	-0.215	-0.034	-0.274	-0.027
-0.033	-0.180	-0.051	-0.125	0.151	0.165	0.097

in the matrix accounted for by the factor. In nontechnical lán-
guage, it can be taken as an indicator of the "importance" of the
factor. As we shall see, factors vary in their "importance" to the
researcher because succeeding factors in an analysis account for
decreasing portions of the variance contained in the original
correlation matrix. At some point, factors may become uninterest-
ing to the analyst because they "explain" too little of the common variance in the matrix.

Accordingly, it was decided that not all factors derived would
be considered for rotation. A common criterion for limiting rotation to "meaningful" factors is the requirement that a factor account for 1/mth of the total variance in the matrix (where m =
the number of variables in the analysis). In the present illustration, the application of this criterion would limit rotation to only
those factors accounting for 1/25th or 4 per cent of the total
variance.[47]

An examination of the ten unrotated factors presented in
Table VII-6 suggests that our criterion for rotation has not caused
us to neglect factors of great importance to our study, because
the last few factors have neither an intelligible structure nor a
large proportion of the variance attached to them. We may recall from the earlier discussion of factor theory that succeeding
factors will account for increasingly smaller portions of the
variance and that increasingly they will represent unique variance components (whether *specific* or *error*) rather than variance shared among other variables in the matrix.

We can now proceed with the preliminary interpretation and
identification of the factors that have been extracted from the
original correlation matrix. No rigid set of steps is used in the
interpretation of factors, but most researchers look first for
variables that load heavily on one factor and do not have high
loadings on other factors. A variable is a good measure of a factor if it has a loading approximating ± 1.0 and has near-zero
loadings on other factors. Since such a situation rarely occurs,
we must compromise and try to find the "purest" measure that
presents itself in the matrix.

For factor 1, the purest measure is variable 2, the Area Re-
development Act. Note that variable 2 has a factor loading of

—.905 on factor 1, and that it does not load heavily on other factors. Other variables with relatively high loadings on the factor are 7, 8, 15, 17, and 18. We must now decipher the common content of these measures; but the diverse nature of the issues appears to belie any underlying issue-orientation. (The roll calls concern issues ranging from the ARA and unemployment compensation to housing, defense expenditures, and the Peace Corps budget.) A clue to interpretation, however, is that nearly all these roll calls dealt with important issues on which the President took a definite stand. Considering only the six variables listed above, we might tentatively suggest that factor 1 reflects support or nonsupport of the President's position, particularly because nearly all the issues opposed by the President have negative loadings on the factor, while most issues supported by the President have positive loadings. Tentatively, we might call this the "Presidential Support" factor.

Factor 2 is simpler to interpret because it does not include as many high loadings as factor 1. Only two variables stand out from the rest—Rule 22 and the vote on the Civil Rights Commission (variables 1 and 20, repectively). Variable 9 (highway expenditures) appears also to be related, but its meaning is not immediately apparent. For the moment, variables 1 and 20 will be accepted as the clearest definitions of factor 2, and we may tentatively identify it as the "Civil Rights" factor.

Factor 3 is illusive and rather difficult to interpret. Variable 4 is a legislative vote on a proposal to extend the Sugar Act of 1948 and to authorize the President to deny a quota bonus to the Dominican Republic because of the cut-back in the importation of Cuban sugar. Variable 13 also shows a moderately high loading on the factor, but its substantive significance is troublesome. It refers to an amendment by Senator Proxmire to cut radiology research funds from the defense appropriation (Proxmire was supported by the President). An inspection of the original correlation matrix shows that variables 4 and 13 have a medium negative correlation of —.44, a higher correlation than either roll call shared with any other roll call in the matrix. In the absence of any additional information that might clarify this relationship, we will entertain the notion that the relationship may be spurious, i.e., simply a matter of chance, of error, or of some influence we have not noted. Since factor 3 accounts for only 6.2 per cent of the variance, the loss of information we suffer by neglecting it may not be crucial to the major portion of our analysis.

Factor 4 accounts for an additional 4.3 per cent of the variance, and its structure is more easily interpreted than that of factor 3. Notice that variable 12 (an amendment to the Agricultural Act to prohibit cooperatives from joining federations) has the highest loading of any variable on that factor. None of the other variables has high loadings on it, and no variable has its highest loading on factor 4. Therefore, we are left with only the single variable (12) as an impure "definition" of this factor. Without further knowledge about related issues, we suggest that this factor reflects the specific influence of one variable: the roll call pertaining to the Agricultural Act. If necessary, we might dub factor 4 an "Agricultural" (or perhaps "Co-op") factor, but its specificity and low contribution of variance offer some justification for ignoring it in subsequent analysis, unless we are particularly interested in agricultural issues.

THE ROTATED FACTOR MATRIX

Factor rotation is designed to "simplify" the relationships detected in the matrix of unrotated factors. According to the criterion of rotation employed in this analysis,[48] the columns of the factor matrix are simplified in such a manner as to maximize the high loadings and minimize the low loadings on a factor. The rotation performed here, then, attempts to "purify" a factor by locating the reference vectors nearest those variables that contribute the greatest proportion of variance to the factor. The substantive importance of rotation to the individual researcher is that rotation usually facilitates interpretation of factors. Research in other disciplines, notably psychology, indicates that rotation may result also in factors that are more stable and more easily comparable from one study to another. Unfortunately, this limited factorial design does not offer any evidence on the question of factor stability, but we can compare the rotated and unrotated solutions in order to see the additional clarity gained by rotation. The matrix of rotated factors is presented in Table VII-7.

TABLE VII-7

R—FACTOR ANALYSIS OF 1961 SENATE ROLL CALL VOTES.

		ROTATED	FACTOR	MATRIX	
SUM SQUARES OVER VARIABLES	FACTOR NUMBER	1 8.837	2 4.380	3 1.780	4 1.555
VARIABLE NO. NAME	COMMUNALITY 4 FACTORS				
1 RULE22	0.737	-0.040	0.854	-0.074	-0.006
2 ARA	0.862	-0.829	0.403	-0.058	-0.091
3 UNEMPL	0.699	-0.777	0.177	-0.253	0.007
4 SUGAR	0.710	-0.095	0.017	0.833	-0.081
5 LABSTN	0.732	-0.415	0.743	-0.019	0.086
6 SCHOOL	0.614	0.629	0.190	-0.089	-0.417
7 INTDEP	0.699	0.820	-0.139	0.014	-0.084
8 HOUSNG	0.717	0.645	-0.532	0.133	0.014
9 $-HWAY	0.494	-0.028	0.675	0.118	-0.155
10 REORG	0.635	-0.779	0.018	-0.163	-0.023
11 E-CEX	0.687	-0.781	0.252	-0.109	0.041
12 AGRACT	0.789	-0.074	-0.066	-0.181	0.864
13 $-IND	0.676	-0.206	-0.106	-0.709	0.346
14 $-HEW	0.676	-0.744	0.053	-0.202	0.281
15 $-DEF	0.797	-0.856	0.245	-0.065	-0.013
16 FORAST	0.474	0.438	-0.436	0.294	0.075
17 MANPOW	0.815	-0.852	0.295	-0.036	-0.032
18 $PEACE	0.739	-0.725	0.316	-0.049	0.333
19 MAJORS	0.621	-0.679	-0.189	-0.019	0.352
20 CIVRTS	0.669	-0.053	0.812	0.062	0.051
21 MERCH	0.385	-0.354	0.054	-0.495	-0.108
22 SBA	0.489	-0.569	0.203	-0.102	0.338
23 ARMCON	0.572	-0.633	0.411	0.009	0.047
24 MEXLAB	0.570	0.484	-0.569	0.066	0.084
25 $-SCHL	0.696	0.580	-0.599	-0.023	0.026

Notice that the communality (h^2) value for each of the variables in the analysis has decreased from the estimates appearing in the unrotated solution. That the communalities in the unrotated matrix referred to a set of ten unrotated factors accounts largely for this fact. Additional loadings of variables on successive factors served to add to the amount of variance contributed to the total factor solution, thus raising the communality estimate for each variable. When a communality estimate is low, we may surmise that the variable holds little in common with the other variables in the design, or we consider the possibility that the variable contributes most of its variance to factors not included in the rotated solution. (Note that the communality for variable 21 is low, suggesting that it is not strongly related to any of the other variables and that it contributes only specific variance to the matrix.)

We can check these possible interpretations of low communalities by examining the successive unrotated factors, if they are available. In our analysis, such an examination indicates that variable 21 contributes fairly large amounts to two factors not included in the rotation. The reader may verify this for himself by referring to the unrotated factor matrix in Table VII-6 (especially factors 5 and 7). The existence of these factors, each of which seems to contain primarily specific variance, bears out the surmise that little of the contributed variance of variable 21 is shared by other variables in the analysis. Generalizing from this example, it might be suggested that, during the interpretation of a rotated solution, a large loss of communality from the unrotated to the rotated matrix may be attributable to the elimination of a more or less specific factor from the final solution.

A further consequence of the rotation procedure, at least for the example given, is that the ratio of the factor sum of squares to the number of variables has been altered. In general, this means that each factor accounts for a proportion of the variance different in the second factor matrix from that in the first. Because the rotation maximized high loadings and minimized low loadings, several variables were weighted more heavily on the second, third, and fourth factors than they were in the unrotated solution. The scope and magnitude of this transferral of variance from one factor to another varies with each analysis, but generally one may expect some change in the variance components attributable to each factor when rotation is performed.

Upon closer inspection of the rotated factor matrix, we find that several variables have decreased their loadings on factor 1 and have gained on succeeding factors. Variable 2 (ARA) has lost variance on factor 1 and has become a less satisfactory definition of that factor. Variable 7, a proposal relating to appropriations for the Department of the Interior, has increased its loading. Variable 10, a Presidential plan for reorganization of the Securities and Exchange Commission, behaved similarly. On the surface, the Presidential involvement in each of these issues suggests that our original interpretation of the factor as one of "Presidential Support" should be retained.

Factor 2 has been simplified and clarified in the rotated matrix. Notice that variable 1 (Rule 22) and variable 20 (Civil Rights Commission) stand out more readily than before. Their loadings have been maximized on factor 2, while their loadings on other factors have been minimized. Two other variables, 5 and 9 (labor standards legislation and highway appropriations) also appear important, although they are by no means "pure" measures of the factors. If they were less ambiguous, we might be tempted to dub this an ideological factor ("Liberal-Conservative," for example); but, for the moment, we shall hold to the interpretation of factor 2 as a "Civil Rights" factor.

To check on the factor rotation and to examine the relationship between factors 1 and 2, we have reproduced the plot of factor loadings for those two factors. Figure VII-12 presents the plot of unrotated factors 1 and 2 against one another; Figure VII-13 presents the plot of the same two factors after rotation. Note how the reference vectors have shifted in their relationship to the positioning of the variables (represented by points, numbered in correspondence to the variable names given elsewhere). Since the plots themselves present the vectors as the abscissa and ordinate (x and y axes) in both plots, it is useful to think of the variables as rotated in a spatial plane while the axes are held steady. This is contrary to the normal interpretation of factor rotation, but it corresponds to the visual presentation of the two plots.

For ease of interpretation, it should be remembered that each point (number) appearing on the plots represents the end of a vector. The position of the point corresponds to its loading on each of the two factors. The magnitude of the loading of each variable can be located on the scale placed along abscissa and ordinate of the plots.

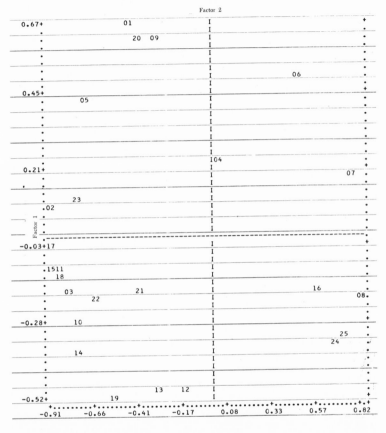

FIGURE VII-12

PLOT OF UNROTATED FACTORS 1 AND 2. R-FACTOR ANALYSIS OF
1961 SENATE ROLL CALL VOTES[*]

* Each number on the plot refers to a variable enumerated in the factor
matrix.

It is worth noting that plotting gives a check also on the ap-
propriateness of the orthogonal rotation. The reference axes are
at 90-degree angles to one another because the rotation we have
performed has forced them to be orthogonal, or uncorrelated.
An inspection of the distribution of points on a plot can indicate

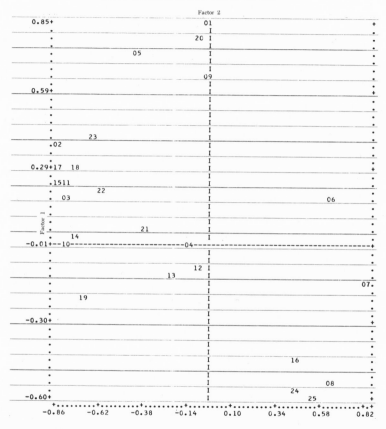

* Each number on the plot refers to a variable enumerated in the factor matrix.

whether this is appropriate or not. In the case of the rotated matrix, it appears that orthogonality is at least partially artificial in our data. If the rotation criterion had allowed the factors to be correlated, the rotation would probably have resulted in a set of obliquely related factor axes (the degree of obliqueness indi-

cating the strength of correlation). This result can be tested by
visual rotation of the abscissa (reference axis for factor 1) clock-
wise until the axis lines up approximately with the diagonal
spread of points in the diagram. Just as John Grumm discovered
that oblique rotation best represented the factors (clusters of
legislators) in his Q-analysis of the Kansas legislature,[49] we
have evidence that an oblique solution might result in a better
representation of this sample of roll-call voting patterns.

Continuing our discussion of the four rotated factors, we can
see that the rotation procedure has simplified the structure of
factors 3 and 4; however, even their simplified nature is of little
use to us. Factor 3 is dominated by variables 4 and 13 as before,
but the substantive significance of this domination is not clear.
Lacking additional information about these issues, we may wish
to exclude this factor from further consideration. Similarly, factor 4 has emerged as a specific factor dominated by the Agricultural Act (variable 12). Because this may result from error in
measurement, or simply from chance, we will want to be cautious
about interpreting this factor. It is worth noting for further
examination, however, that agricultural issues may constitute an
independent dimension of conflict in the United States Senate.

Summarizing briefly, it appears that we have tentatively uncovered four factors relating to conflict in the Senate. The first
two factors, accounting for 35.3 per cent and 17.5 per cent of
the variance in the *rotated* factor matrix, appear to be characterized by conflict over presidential support and civil rights.
The second two factors, accounting for 7.1 per cent and 6.2 per
cent of the variance, are of less over-all importance, but they may
suggest possible relationships to be followed up in another
analysis. Factor 4 might be of particular interest because it suggests that conflict over agricultural issues may exist relatively
independently. In both situations, we have found factor analysis
of use—in the case of the first two factors, we have described
some of the major conflict dimensions in the Senate; in the case
of the second two, we found some suggestions for further analysis
and hypothesis-testing. Both outcomes are fruitful and legitimate
uses of factor analysis.

ANALYSIS OF FACTOR SCORES

We have suggested that factor scores can be used to plot the positions of individual legislators (or for that matter, nations in the UN, or labor unions in the International Labor Organization) along the dimensions uncovered in the R-factor analysis of legislative voting. This use of factor scores is analogous to the interpretation of factor loadings in a Q-analysis of the same data.[50] In our R-analysis, the dimensions (factors) refer not to individuals, as in Q-technique, but to issues. If the factors represent valid and theoretically meaningful dimensions of behavior, however, it is useful to use factor scores to place individuals along those dimensions. Although we will not attempt to carry out a full-scale cluster analysis, a few illustrations of its potential utility will be made with simple distributions.

Table VII-8 suggests the gross distribution of "Presidential Support" scores for the 101 senators who voted on issues included in this analysis (recall that Tower replaced Blakley during the session). Note the strong influence of party affiliation on the over-all distribution.

TABLE VII-8

"PRESIDENTIAL SUPPORT" SCORES OF SENATORS IN THE 1961 SESSION
OF THE UNITED STATES SENATE

"Presidential Support"	Party		
	Democrat	Republican	
above zero	52	0	52
below zero	13	36	49
	65	36	101

The split in the Democratic party along this dimension of conflict in the 1961 Senate is explicated further in Table VII-9, which classifies Democrats as Southern or non-Southern (included in the former category are senators from Alabama, Arkansas, Florida, Georgia, Louisiana, Mississippi, North Carolina, South Carolina, Texas, and Virginia).

TABLE VII-9

"PRESIDENTIAL SUPPORT" AMONG DEMOCRATIC SENATORS IN THE
1961 SESSION OF THE UNITED STATES SENATE, CLASSIFIED BY REGION

Region

"Presidential
Support"

	Non-South	South	
above zero	43	9	52
below zero	2	11	13
	45	20	65

This table implies that Southern Democratic senators support the leader of their party less strongly than do Democrats from other parts of the country. This implication holds even when much of the influence of "Civil Rights" has been factored out and concentrated in factor 2. If our analysis indicates reality, we apparently have a trace of the "conservative coalition," in which Southern Democrats may join forces with Northern Republicans to oppose a liberal administration. Apparently, the dimension of "Presidential Support" is complicated by ideological considerations. On the other hand, it appears that several Southerners give strong support to party and President when civil rights and filibustering (Rule 22) are removed. (The reader is invited to examine the Appendix to this chapter for the rank ordering of senators on this dimension. The ranking itself may be instructive, but the existence of certain apparent discrepancies offers an opportunity for deviant-case analysis and also serves as a caution about the use of factor scores.)

These tables, though they convey no startling information about Senate voting patterns, do indicate that factor scores can yield a solution that conforms to interpretations gained from other approaches. To be sure, one does not need factor analysis to learn that Southern Democrats tend to oppose a liberal Administration more than non-Southern Democrats do. Nevertheless, factor analysis as used in this example not only can describe the major dimensions in voting behavior, but it can also yield scales along which individuals can be ranked. The possibilities of such an approach go far beyond the simple demonstrations presented here.

A more elaborate analysis than the simple cross-classifications we have presented would probably use finer cutting points on the full range of factor scores, perhaps dividing the scores into quartiles or deciles.[51] Another possible technique might correlate the factor scores of individuals with other variables considered relevant to the dimension underlying the scale.[52] Still another possible application might use factor scores as dependent or independent variables in multiple regression and correlation designs.[53] With a little imagination, this valuable source of data can be used in a variety of ways to expand the scope of the factor analysis.

CONCLUSION

This *R*-technique factor analysis has illustrated factorial methods in the treatment of legislative voting patterns. The quality of information obtained through factor analysis, as through any other statistical method, depends on the quality of the data used, and on the ability of the researcher to select and interpret. Factor analysis will not produce miraculous new insights about legislative behavior, but it can describe the structure of legislative voting and relate individuals to that structure.

Because a factorial solution depends on the variables included in the analysis, it is necessary for the investigator to exercise certain controls over his data. Indiscriminate selection of sample variables can result in a considerable amount of wasted effort expended by both people and machines. If, for example, many of the roll calls in our sample had been duplicated, certain issue areas might have swamped the factor structure, giving a misleading picture' of actual conflict dimensions in the Senate. On the other hand, our selection of only non-duplicated, "significant" roll calls probably built certain possibly undesirable characteristics into the factor structure we obtained, such as lack of differentiation between ideology and Presidential support, or the correlation between the "Presidential Support" and "Civil Rights" factors. In general, then, it should be remembered that any factor solution is the product of the initial selection process, which itself may color the results.[54]

APPENDIX

RANK ORDERING OF UNITED STATES SENATORS ON THE "PRESIDENTIAL SUPPORT" SCALE FOR THE 1961 SESSION. BASED ON ROTATED FACTOR SCORES DERIVED FROM THE R-ANALYSIS OF SELECTED ROLL-CALL VOTES

1. Kefauver (D-Tenn.)
2. Gore (D-Tenn.)
3. Bible (D-Nev.)
4. Byrd (D-W. Va.)
5. Hill (D-Ala.)
6. Long (D-Hawaii)
7. Mansfield (D-Montana)
8. Church (D-Idaho)
9. Fulbright (D-Ark.)
10. Clark (D-Pa.)
11. Johnston (D-S.C.)
12. Sparkman (D-Ala.)
13. McGee (D-Wyo.)
14. Long (D-La.)
15. Yarborough (D-Tex.)
16. Young (D-Ohio)
17. Metcalf (D-Montana)
18. Hickey (D-Wyo.)
19. Monroney (D-Okla.)
20. Bartlett (D-Alaska)
21. Moss (D-Utah)
22. Morse (D-Ore.)
23. McNamara (D-Mich.)
24. Carroll (D-Colo.)
25. Gruening (D-Alaska)
26. Humphrey (D-Minn.)
27. Anderson (D-N.M.)
28. Randolph (D-W. Va.)
29. Cannon (D-Nev.)
30. Hayden (D-Ariz.)
31. Burdick (D-N.D.)
32. Pastore (D-R.I.)
33. Pell (D-R.I.)
34. Engle (D-Calif.)
35. Jackson (D-Wash.)
36. Neuberger (D-Ore.)
37. Douglas (D-Ill.)
38. Williams (D-N.J.)
39. Hart (D-Mich.)
40. McCarthy (R-Minn.)
41. Hartke (D-Ind.)
42. Kerr (D-Okla.)
43. Magnuson (D-Wash.)
44. Symington (D-Mo.)
45. Smith (D-Mass.)
46. Muskie (D-Me.)
47. Proxmire (D-Wis.)
48. Long (D-Mo.)

49. Talmadge (D-Ga.)
50. Blakley (D-Tex.)
51. Chavez (D-N.M.)
52. Eastland (D-Miss.)

—*zero point*—

53. Ellender (D-La.)
54. Dodd (D-Conn.)
55. Russell (D-Ga.)
56. Bridges (R-N.H.)
57. Jordan (D-N.C.)
58. Smathers (D-Fla.)
59. Javits (R-N.Y.)
60. Stennis (D-Miss.)
61. Case (R-N.J.)
62. Ervin (D-N.C.)
63. Carlson (R-Kansas)
64. Wiley (R-Wis.)
65. Butler (R-Md.)
66. Byrd (D-Va.)
67. Tower (R-Tex.)
68. McClellan (D-Ark.)
69. Boggs (R-Del.)
70. Schoeppel (R-Kansas)
71. Cooper (R-Ky.)
72. Thurmond (D-S.C.)
73. Curtis (R-Neb.)

74. Cotton (R-N.H.)
75. Goldwater (R-Ariz.)
76. Holland (D-Fla.)
77. Dirksen (R-Ill.)
78. Dworshak (R-Idaho)
79. Robertson (D-Va.)
80. Miller (R-Iowa)
81. Aiken (R-Vt.)
82. Hruska (D-Neb.)
83. Williams (R-Del.)
84. Scott (R-Pa.)
85. Young (R-N.D.)
86. Case (R-S.D.)
87. Allott (R-Colo.)
88. Mundt (R-S.D.)
89. Capehart (R-Ind.)
90. Morton (R-Ky.)
91. Saltonstall (R-Mass.)
92. Bush (R-Conn.)
93. Hickenlooper (R-Iowa)
94. Keating (R-N.Y.)
95. Fong (R-Hawaii)
96. Prouty (R-Vt.)
97. Bennett (R-Utah)
98. Lausche (D-Ohio)
99. Beall (R-Md.)
100. Kuchel (R-Calif.)
101. Smith (R-Me.)

NOTES

[1] Major references on factor analysis include the following: Sir Godfrey Thomson, *The Factorial Analysis of Human Ability* (Boston: Houghton Mifflin, 1939); L. L. Thurstone, *Multiple-Factor Analysis* (Chicago: University of Chicago Press, 1947); Raymond B. Cattell, *Factor Analysis* (New York: Harper & Row, 1952); C. J. Adcock, *Factorial Analysis for Non-Mathematicians* (Carlton, Victoria: Melbourne University Press, 1954); Benjamin Fruchter, *Introduction to Factor Analysis* (Princeton, New Jersey: Van Nostrand, 1954); J. P. Guilford, *Psychometric Methods* (New York: McGraw-Hill, 1954); Harry Harman, *Modern Factor Analysis* (Chicago: University of Chicago Press, 1960); D. N. Lawley and A. E. Maxwell, *Factor Analysis as a Statistical Method* (London: Butterworth, 1963).

[2] See, for example, Calvin Hall and Gardner Lindzey, *Theories of Personality* (New York: John Wiley & Sons, 1957).

[3] See, for example, the studies cited in Rudolph Rummel, *Applied Factor Analysis* (Evanston, Illinois: Northwestern University Press, forthcoming).

[4] Hilding B. Carlson and Willard Harrell, "Voting Groups Among Leading Congressmen Obtained by Means of the Inverted Factor Technique," *Journal of Social Psychology*, 16 (August, 1942), 51-61.

[5] Chester W. Harris, "A Factor Analysis of Selected Roll Calls, 80th Congress," *Educational and Psychological Measurement*, 8 (Winter, 1948), 583-91.

[6] John G. Grumm, "A Factor Analysis of Legislative Behavior," *Midwest Journal of Political Science*, 7 (November, 1963), 336-56.

[7] See the section on interpretation of factors, page 000.

[8] Hayward R. Alker, Jr., "Dimensions of Conflict in the General Assembly," *American Political Science Review*, 58 (September, 1964), 642-57.

[9] Terminology varies here according to discipline and author: variables are otherwise called traits, tests, characteristics, etc.; units are entities, individuals, cases, etc.

[10] Variance is a standard statistical measure of the degree of dispersion of the values of a variable. Its value is given by the following formula:

$$\text{Variance} = \frac{\sum_{i=1}^{n} (X_i - \overline{X})^2}{N}$$

where X_i = the score of individual i, and

$\overline{X}$ = the mean score of the N individuals.

[11] Correlation matrices are a typical starting point for factor analysis and serve well as an introduction to the method. As a mathematical model, however, factor analysis can be applied to a variety of matrices, including a raw data matrix. See Rummel (forthcoming), *op. cit.*

[12] This interpretation holds except for the values in the principal diagonal (r_{11}, r_{22}, etc.), which are the correlations of the variables with themselves and are therefore always 1.0. A correlation is a statistical measure of the degree or strength of relationship between two variables. See Hubert M. Blalock, Jr., *Social Statistics* (New York: McGraw-Hill, 1960), Chapter 17.

[13] This notation follows Fruchter, *op. cit.*, p. 47.

[14] The reliability coefficient, r_{jj}, represents a proportion of variance and need not be squared as do the other symbols in the formula.

[15] Correlated factors are called *oblique* factors.

[16]Much of the theory of factor analysis is expressed in terms of matrix algebra; however, a presentation of matrix concepts would complicate this chapter unnecessarily. For more information, see Fruchter, *op. cit.*; Harman, *op. cit.*; and Paul Horst, *Matrix Algebra for Social Scientists* (New York: Holt, Rinehart and Winston, 1963).

[17]For an interesting discussion of the geometric concepts involved here, see Yrjo Ahmavaara and Touko Markkanen, *The Unified Factor Model* (Helsinki: The Finnish Foundation for Alcohol Studies, Volume No. 7, 1957).

[18]The final geometric construct is called an n-dimensional hypersphere.

[19]See Thurstone, *op. cit.*, p. 90, for a proof of this equation.

[20]Here the vector lengths are irrelevant, for the cosine of a 90-degree angle equals 0.

[21]When dealing with factor structures of more than two dimensions, researchers often examine visually a pair of factors at a time on two-dimensional graphs or plots. These are illustrated later in the chapter.

[22]Cattell, *op. cit.*, p. 37.

[23]See Fruchter, *op. cit.*, pp. 59-84, and Guilford, *op. cit.*, pp. 485-500, for computational procedures for the centroid method of factoring, probably the most important method that can realistically be used without computers. Harman, *op. cit.*, Chapter 6, presents a useful systematic comparison of the various methods of extraction.

[24]Guilford, *op. cit.*, p. 494.

[25]See Fruchter, *op. cit.*, pp. 51-52; Harman, *op. cit.*; and William W. Cooley and Paul R. Lohnes, *Multivariate Procedures for the Behavioral Sciences* (Englewood Cliffs, N. J.: Prentice-Hall, 1962), pp. 159-60.

[26]See Andrew L. Comrey and E. Levonian, "A Comparison of Three Point Coefficients in Factor Analysis of MMPI Items," *Educational and Psychological Measurement*, 18 (1958), 739-55; Carl D. McMurray, "Some Problems in the Application of Factor Analytic Techniques to Roll Call Votes, Judicial Decisions, and Survey Responses," delivered at the 1964 Annual Meeting of The American Political Science Association, Chicago, Illinois, September 9-12, 1964; and J. P. Guilford, "The Minimal Phi Coefficient and the Maximal Phi," *Educational and Psychological Measurement*, 25 (Spring, 1965), 3-8.

[27]See Carl D. McMurray, "A Factor Method for Roll Call Studies," *American Behavioral Scientist*, 6 (April, 1963), 26-27; Hayward R. Alker, Jr., *op. cit.*; and Alker, "Dimensions of Voting in the United Nations," (unpublished doctoral dissertation, Yale University, 1963).

[28]See Harman, *op. cit.*; Lawley and Maxwell, *op. cit.*, pp. 92-101; Yrjo Ahmavaara, *Transformation Analysis of Factorial Data* (Helsinki, 1954); and Raymond B. Cattell, "The Basis of Recognition

and Interpretation of Factors," *Educational and Psychological Measurement*, 22 (Winter, 1962), 667-98.

[29]Thurstone, *op. cit.*, p. 335.

[30]See Fruchter, *op. cit.*, pp. 113-14.

[31]See Fruchter, *op. cit.*, pp. 194-96; Harman, *op. cit.*; and R. W. Coan, "Facts, Factors, and Artifacts: The Quest for Psychological Meaning," *Psychological Review*, 71 (March, 1964), 123-40.

[32]The term *factor* is thus, with some confusion, used variably to refer to (1) the statistical concept and (2) the theoretical concept.

[33]See Richard W. Coan, "Facts, Factors, and Artifacts: The Quest for Psychological Meaning," *loc. cit.*, 123-40; H. J. Eysenck, "The Logical Basis of Factor Analysis," *American Psychologist*, 8 (1953), 105-14; and Rudolph Rummel, *op. cit.*

[34]For a brief but interesting note on these two models, see Hubert M. Blalock, Jr., *Causal Inferences in Nonexperimental Research* (Chapel Hill: The University of North Carolina Press, 1964). The first chapter of this book contains a compact discussion of the rationale behind causal thinking.

[35]For a good summary discussion, see A. Cornelius Benjamin, *Operationism* (Springfield, Illinois: Thomas, 1955).

[36]See the interesting discussion on measurement in James Coleman, *Introduction to Mathematical Sociology* (New York: The Free Press, 1964).

[37]Julius Turner, *Party and Constituency: Pressures on Congress* (Baltimore: Johns Hopkins Studies in Historical and Political Science, 1951).

[38]For examples of factor interpretation, see Fruchter, *op. cit.*, pp. 155-91; and William W. Cooley and Paul R. Lohnes, *op. cit.*, pp. 154-57 and 164-72.

[39]Benjamin Fruchter, "Factor Analysis," in Harold Borko (ed.), *Computer Applications in the Behavioral Sciences* (Englewood Cliffs, N.J.: Prentice-Hall, 1962), Chapter 11, pp. 260-62.

[40]For discussions of these techniques and of others, see Fruchter, *op. cit.*, pp. 202-204; Raymond B. Cattell, "The Three Basic Factor-Analytic Research Designs—Their Interrelations and Derivatives," *Psychological Bulletin*, 49 (1952), 499-520; and R. W. Coan, "Basic Forms of Covariation and Concomitance Designs," *Psychological Bulletin*, 58 (July, 1961), 317-24.

[41]This means that the cards used in computer programs may have to be transposed, with each card or set of cards representing a variable rather than a unit, or vice versa. If a standard transposition program is not available, a special program can be written with little difficulty.

[42]Arguments over the relationships between R and Q analyses are contained and referenced in Donald M. Broverman, "Effects of Score Transformations in Q and R Factor Analysis Techniques,"

Psychological Review, 68 (January, 1961), 68-80, and John Ross, "The Relation between Test and Person Factors," *Psychological Review*, 70 (September, 1963), 432-43.

[43]The actual data for this analysis was obtained from the data archives of the Interuniversity Consortium for Political Research. Without the assistance of the ICPR, the original analyses carried out in this book would have been much more costly in time and effort.

[44]McMurray, *op. cit.* Another relevant work by the same author is, "Using the Computer to Identify Legislators' Voting Patterns on Roll-Call Votes," Tallahassee: Institute of Governmental Research and Department of Government, The Florida State University, April, 1963).

[45]Carl D. McMurray discusses this problem in his paper, "Some Problems in The Application of Factor Analytic Techniques to Roll Call Votes, Judicial Decisions, and Survey Response," presented at the 1964 Annual Meeting of The American Political Science Association, September, 1964.

[46]*Ibid.*

[47]In technical language, $1/m$th of the variance is called an "eigenvalue." From this it follows that the sum of the squared factor loadings (discussed above) equals the number of eigenvalues associated with a factor. To obtain the amount of variance *actually* accounted for by a factor, multiply the *number* of eigenvalues by the percentage of variance associated with one eigenvalue. In this example, the amount of variance accounted for by factor 1 is 10.798 x 4% = 43.2%. The values for the succeeding three factors are 12.5%, 6.2%, and 4.3% (giving a total of 66.2% for the first four factors).

[48]We have used the "varimax" criterion of factor rotation. For a technical exposition of this technique, see the following articles by Henry Kaiser: "Computer Program for Varimax Rotation in Factor Analysis," *Educational and Psychological Measurement*, 19 (Autumn, 1959), 413-20; and "The Varimax Criterion for Analytical Rotation in Factor Analysis," *Psychometrika*, 23 (September, 1958), 187-200.

[49]John G. Grumm, *op. cit.*, pp. 336-56.

[50]The comparison between R-technique and Q-technique is not quite as simple as it is stated here, but the argument about the logical and mathematical comparability of the two approaches is beyond the scope of this presentation. For a more detailed background, the reader is referred to: Jack Block, "The Difference Between R and Q," *Psychological Review*, 62 (1955), 356-58; and Raymond B. Cattell, "The Three Basic Factor-Analytic Research Designs—Their Interrelations and Their Deviations," *loc. cit.*

[51]Carl D. McMurray has suggested a scaling procedure of this type in his paper, "Using the Computer to Identify Voting Patterns on Roll Call Votes," *loc. cit.* For a more recent discussion of this pro-

cedure and an example of its use, see Carl D. McMurray and Malcolm B. Parsons, "Public Attitudes Toward the Representational Role of Legislators and Judges." *Midwest Journal of Political Science*, 9 (May, 1965), 167-85.

[52]John Grumm, in "A Factor Analysis of Legislative Behavior," *loc. cit.*, uses rank-order statistics and biserial correlations to relate individual scores in his Q-analysis to various personal and constituency characteristics. Also, since the factor scores are ostensibly in interval form, the Pearson product-moment correlation coefficient could be used in this context.

[53]Hayward R. Alker, Jr., has made interesting use of multiple regression methods to relate environmental variables to positions on United Nations conflict dimensions (*op. cit.*). In the same article, he uses factor scores to plot the positions of nations (cluster-type analysis) and to correlate conflict positions with "constituency" variables and group membership. On the use of advanced correlation and regression techniques, the reader may wish to refer to Andrew R. Baggaley, *Intermediate Correlational Methods* (New York: John Wiley and Sons, Inc., 1964); and to Mordecai Ezekiel and Karl A. Fox, *Methods of Correlation and Regression Analysis,* third edition, (New York: John Wiley and Sons, Inc., 1959).

[54]Glendon Schubert has developed a complex psychometric model of judicial behavior which involves the use of both Guttman scaling and factor analysis. See Glendon Schubert, "A Solution to the Indeterminant Factorial Resolution of Thurstone and Degan's Study of the Supreme Court," *Behavioral Science*, 7 (October, 1962), 448-458; "A Psychometric Model of the Supreme Court," *American Behavioral Scientist*, 5 (November, 1961), 14-18; "Psychometric Research in Judicial Behavior", *Modern Uses of Logic in Law*, 2 (March, 1962), 9-18; "1960-61 Term of the Supreme Court: A Psychological Analysis," *American Political Science Review*, 56 (March, 1962) 90-107; "Psychometric Analysis of Judicial Behavior: The 1961 Term of the Supreme Court," *Law and Contemporary Problems*, 28 (Winter, 1963); and *The Judicial Mind: The Attitudes and Ideologies of Supreme Court Justices* (Evanston: Northwestern University Press, 1965).

CHAPTER VIII

SOME COMPUTER PROGRAMS
USEFUL IN ROLL-CALL ANALYSIS

We have noted that the coming of electronic data-processing equipment has contributed substantially to the growth of research on legislative voting. Most of the methods of analysis described in this book can be executed on computers, and some of them, such as cluster-bloc analysis and factor analysis, require computer executions. In this chapter, we shall describe some computer routines that are particularly useful in roll-call voting research. Some of these programs have been written especially for this book. The others mentioned are available in writings on computer programming.

PROGRAMS WRITTEN ESPECIALLY FOR THIS BOOK

The four computer programs discussed in this section were written to carry out the manipulation of legislative roll calls in cases in which the votes have been stored on punch cards[1] for analysis. For each of these programs, we shall give a general description of the program and its applications; instructions on the preparation of cards for processing; a listing of the actual Fortran language statements that make up the program; and a sample of output from the program. The interested reader who has a computer at his disposal may punch the statements directly from this book and, following the appropriate instructions, may put the routines to his own use. If the potential user is not sufficiently familiar with the language and technique of programming, he may be able to engage someone from a computer laboratory to perform the relatively simple operations needed for these programs. Two cautions, however, should be offered.

First, these programs are given in the Fortran computing language[2] as used by the Control Data Corporation's 3400 series computer. The elements of this version of Fortran are nearly the same as those of the more commonly used Fortran II and IV. Only a few statements need be altered to make the programs compatible on other systems (the IBM 7090, for example). Nevertheless, certain conventions will doubtless vary from system to system, and the user should have the programs checked by a competent programmer before he attempts to run problems with them.[3]

Secondly, the programs are designed to fit the demands of the investigator who is studying a two-party American legislature, primarily the United States Congress. No claim is made that the programs ACCUM and CORR can be applied to all legislatures, and it should be clear that they do not. The VOTES program, however, can derive significance coefficients for votes in any legislative system and is therefore more generally applicable.

ACCUM: COMPUTER ROUTINE FOR THE ACCUMULATION OF MARGINAL TOTALS AND THE COMPUTATION OF SIMPLE INDEX VALUES

Program ACCUM is designed to facilitate the preliminary analysis and manipulation of legislative roll-call votes that have been stored on punch cards by individual vote. This means that data have been recorded on cards, each card representing an individual and the values punched in the columns of the card recording voting positions he has taken. Recorded in this fashion, the data for the study will constitute a file of punch cards in which a card or set of cards contains the responses of a single legislator for all roll calls considered relevant. There will be as many cards (or sets of cards) as there are legislators.

The program will read in a set of data and place it in a matrix like the following:

VOTES

	1,1	1,2	1,3	.	.	.	1,J
L	2,1	2,2	2,3	.	.	.	2,J
E	3,1	3,2	3,3	.	.	.	3,J
G	.	.	.				.
I	.	.	.				.
S	.	.	.				.
L	.	.	.				.
A	.	.	.				.
T	.	.	.				.
O	.	.	.				.
R	.	.	.				.
S	.	.	.				.
	I,1	I,2	I,3	.	.	.	I,J

where: I = the number of legislators, and
J = the number of roll calls.

The data is accumulated by columns, each column representing one roll call, to obtain totals for each individual vote.

The output of the program is as follows:

1. The division of the vote by party (i.e., total "yeas" and "nays" for Democrats and Republicans).
2. A total division of the vote.
3. A Rice Index of Cohesion for each party on each vote.[4]
4. An Index of Party Likeness for each roll-call vote.[5]
5. A coefficient of significance for the vote.[6]

The general utility of this program is that it can provide a profile of each legislative vote that is processed, including measures of group conflict and cohesion. The marginal totals provide a check on the division of the vote and can be used to check the accuracy with which the votes have been punched on cards. (If the marginal totals are elsewhere available, the accumulation program will indicate whether there is error in the data.)

Output from the ACCUM program is printed in the form given in the sample output shown in Figure VIII-1. When desired, the program will also generate a profile card for each roll call on which the above information is recorded. The punch-card output is particularly useful when one wishes to record such data as the Rice Index, the Index of Party Likeness, and the coefficient of significance for further analysis. Each roll call processed in the program will be numbered in the order in which it is treated by the machine; thus, identification numbers will be given consecutively to each vote in the order processed.

The instructions below should enable the user to prepare data for processing with the ACCUM program.

Order of Cards for Input:
> System cards (specific to each computer installation)
> Fortran source program
> Input format statement (1)*
> Problem card (1)**
> Data cards
> End card***

*Variables to read in are:
1. The party identification of the legislator (1 = Democrat; 2 = Republican). I-format (1) to be used.
2. Voting responses on roll calls (1 = "yea"; 2 = "nay"). I-format (1) to be used.

The party identification of an individual must appear before any of his responses to votes.

**The problem card is punched as follows:

Columns
1-4   Number of legislators for which responses occur in the data (may exceed size of legislature because of replacements).
5   blank
6-9   Number of roll calls to be processed. Total should be right-adjusted with leading zeroes punched; e.g., 0050 where 50 roll calls are being processed (up to a maximum of 45 unless special provisions noted under "limitations" are made).
10   blank
11-14 Size of the legislature.

15   blank
16-19 Size of a quorum in the legislature.
20   blank
21   Option for punch card output (1 = punch; 0 = no punch).

***The end card signals the end of all data to be processed during one run of the program. It contains six nines (999999), in columns 1-6. This card follows the last data card.

If more than one set of data is to be processed during the same computer run, the format statement for the second batch of data immediately follows the last data card of the preceding problem. As many sets of data may be processed as the researcher desires.

When *multiple problems* are processed, the order of cards will be as follows:

System cards
Fortran source statement
Input format statement for 1st subset of data
Problem card for 1st subset of data
Data cards
Input format statement for 2nd subset of data
Problem card for 2nd set of data
Data cards
  *   *   *
Input format statement for last subset of data
Problem card for last subset of data
Data cards
End card

The primary purpose of multiple-problem processing in this fashion is to allow inclusion of a full set of roll calls belonging to one analysis. Since machine capacity is limited, the option is provided for the analysis of successive sets of data. Because this feature is intended primarily to permit segmentation of a set of roll calls into several subsets for processing, each roll call processed at one time will be numbered consecutively, regardless of the way in which roll calls are split into subsets.

LIMITATIONS

The standard ACCUM source program will handle roll-call votes (up to 45) where the size of the legislature does not exceed 450. If either total should exceed these figures, the program user should modify the routine as follows:

Figure VIII-1

SAMPLE OUTPUT OF ACCUM PROGRAM

BILL ID	DEMS		COHESION	REPS	
	YEAS	NAYS		YEAS	NAYS
1	32	31	1.6	18	15
2	9	48	68.4	9	18
3	48	8	71.4	19	10
4	41	8	67.3	11	18
5	16	47	49.2	29	2
6	3	57	90.0	29	4
7	3	57	90.0	24	9
8	2	57	93.2	17	14
9	13	47	56.7	23	8
10	4	53	86.0	27	4
11	48	11	62.7	15	16
12	59	0	100.0	31	1
13	48	11	62.7	24	7
14	16	39	41.8	26	5
15	25	33	13.8	26	5
16	14	42	50.0	31	0
17	55	2	93.0	29	2
18	48	7	74.5	19	6
19	47	9	67.9	11	22
20	0	50	100.0	31	0
21	0	52	100.0	29	1
22	7	48	74.5	10	20
23	35	22	22.8	20	12
24	10	53	68.3	24	10
25	14	50	56.3	20	13
26	14	49	55.6	21	13
27	9	54	71.4	30	4
28	15	46	50.8	24	9
29	20	43	36.5	19	13
30	21	42	33.3	24	10
31	51	11	64.5	14	17
32	48	13	57.4	16	15
33	54	3	89.5	32	2
34	48	2	92.0	15	15
35	8	47	70.9	20	7
36	36	18	33.3	7	18
37	60	0	100.0	32	0
38	19	44	39.7	6	26
39	14	47	54.1	16	17
40	0	61	100.0	0	34
41	11	49	63.3	18	14
42	12	49	60.7	10	24
43	10	43	62.3	23	7
44	54	4	86.2	7	21
45	42	18	40.0	9	21

COHESION	TOTAL		IPL	COEFFICIENT
	YEAS	NAYS		OF SIGNIF.
9.1	50	46	96	0.9323
33.3	18	66	82	0.4755
31.0	67	18	80	0.4758
24.1	52	26	54	0.5407
87.1	45	49	32	0.9050
75.8	32	61	17	0.7180
45.5	27	66	32	0.6513
9.7	19	71	49	0.5305
48.4	36	55	47	0.7575
74.2	31	57	20	0.6767
3.2	63	27	67	0.6372
93.8	90	1	97	0.2906
54.8	72	18	96	0.5171
67.7	42	44	45	0.8096
67.7	51	38	59	0.7703
100.0	45	42	25	0.8098
87.1	84	4	97	0.3165
52.0	67	13	89	0.3811
33.3	58	31	49	0.6770
100.0	31	50	0	0.6215
93.3	29	53	3	0.6084
33.3	17	68	79	0.4625
25.0	55	34	99	0.7170
41.2	34	63	45	0.7724
21.2	34	63	61	0.7724
23.5	35	62	60	0.7858
76.5	39	58	26	0.8391
45.5	39	55	52	0.8250
18.8	39	56	72	0.8253
41.2	45	52	63	0.9192
9.7	65	28	63	0.6647
3.2	64	28	73	0.6644
88.2	86	5	99	0.3440
0.0	63	17	54	0.4345
48.1	28	54	40	0.5951
44.0	43	36	61	0.6743
100.0	92	0	100	0.2909
62.5	25	70	89	0.6385
3.0	30	64	74	0.7049
100.0	0	95	100	0.3050
12.5	29	63	62	0.6777
41.2	22	73	90	0.5985
53.3	33	50	42	0.6620
50.0	61	25	32	0.5828
40.0	51	39	60	0.7973

Remove the DIMENSION statement—identified by "AC-CUM060" in columns 73-80 of the Fortran card.

Prepare a new DIMENSION statement, entering the appropriate totals for the data deck. For example, if the legislature has 100 members and 250 roll calls are to be processed, the modified statement should be:

DIMENSION IBILL (100,250), IPARTY (100).

In no case, however, should the product of the two variable sums exceed 32,768 when used on the IBM 709 computer or unit of similar capacity. (Remember also that the DIMENSION statement should begin in column 7 of the card.)

The actual Fortran listing of program ACCUM appears in Figure VIII-2.

VOTES: A COMPUTER PROGRAM FOR DERIVING COEFFICIENTS OF SIGNIFICANCE

VOTES, a Fortran program, computes significance coefficients (according to the formulas of William H. Riker) for a series of legislative roll-call votes for which the marginal totals ("yeas" and "nays") are stored on punch cards, one card per roll call. The set of roll calls processed at one time will be rank-ordered in descending order of "significance." If desired, the coefficients can be punched on cards (one card per roll call). On the printed and punched output, each roll call will be assigned a number from 1 to N (where N = the total number of roll calls processed), according to the rank-ordering of the corresponding coefficient of significance. Sample output for the VOTES program appears in Table VII-6, page 155.

The VOTES program will be useful when the user wishes to obtain significance coefficients without first accumulating individual responses. In fact, this program can be used to select roll calls that might later be recorded by individual response.

Order of cards for input:

System cards
Fortran source program
Input format statement for data*

Problem card**
Data cards

*Variables to be read in the format card are the following:

1. Bill identification number (up to four integers).
2. Number on the "yea" side of the issue.
3. Number on the "nay" side of the issue.

The ID number will be read in using I-format. Marginal totals will be in F-format.

Example format: (I4,4X,F4.0,5X,F4.0)

**The problem card is arranged as follows:

Columns

1-4   Sample size, i.e., number of roll calls being processed. Number should be right-adjusted, with leading zeroes punched. (Maximum = 1000.)
5   blank
6-9   Size of the legislature. Right-adjusted, with leading zeroes punched.
10   blank
11-14 Size of a quorum for the legislature, e.g., 0051 for the U.S. Senate, 0219 for the House.
20   Option for punch card output (1 = punch; 0 = no punch).

The formulas for the coefficient of significance apply only to roll calls decided on the basis of a simple majority. If a particular vote refers to a procedural vote in which an extraordinary majority (say two-thirds) occurs, the program will nevertheless calculate the coefficient on the basis of a simple majority. For this reason, votes requiring more than the usual majority for passage should be removed from the original computer analysis and reserved for a special run in which the extraordinary majority can be specified on the problem card. For example, the size of a quorum in the United States Senate would normally be punched as 0051 on the problem card; an extraordinary majority would be punched as 0067.

The Fortran listing for program VOTES appears in Figure VIII-3.

Figure VIII-2

FORTRAN LANGUAGE LISTING OF ACCUM PROGRAM

```
      PROGRAM ACCUM
C PROGRAM FOR ACCUMULATING MARGINAL FREQUENCIES WHERE DATA IS STORED
C BY INDIVIDUAL VOTE. SUBTOTALS AND A RICE INDEX OF COHESION ARE
C CALCULATED FOR EACH PARTY.  AN INDEX OF PARTY LIKENESS AND COEFFICIENT
C OF SIGNIFICANCE ALSO GIVEN.
      COMMON/1/IBILL,IPARTY,FMT
      DIMENSION IBILL(450,45), IPARTY (450)
      DIMENSION FMT(12)
      EQUIVALENCE (FMT(1),NFMT)
      NTEST = 999999
      ID = 1
C READ FORMAT CARD
 1000 READ(60,33)(FMT(I), I=1,12)
   33 FORMAT (12A6)
C TEST FOR END CARD. IF NOT, CONTINUE EXECUTION.
      IF (NFMT - NTEST) 37,2000,37
C SET CORE = 0
   37 DO 1 I=1,N
      DO 1 J=1,NV
      IPARTY (I) = 0
      IBILL (I,J) = 0
    1 CONTINUE
C READ CONTROL CARD
      READ (60,34) N,NV,SIZE,QUOR,IPUNCH
   34 FORMAT (I4,1X,I4,1X,F4.0,1X,F4.0,1X,I1)
C READ DATA ACCORDING TO FORMAT
      READ (60,FMT) (IPARTY(I),(IBILL(I,J), J=1,NV), I=1,N)
      WRITE (61,61)
   61 FORMAT (1H1,5X,7HBILL ID,9X,4HDEMS,8X,8HCOHESION,8X,4HREPS,8X,
     18HCOHESION,8X,5HTOTAL,8X,3HIPL,8X,11HCOEFFICIENT//17X,4HYEAS,4X,4H
     2NAYS,16X,4HYEAS,4X,4HNAYS,16X,4HYEAS,5X,4HNAYS,15X,10HOF SIGNIF,/)
    4 CONTINUE
      DO 105 J=1,NV
      IDEMY = 0
      IDEMN = 0
      IREPY = 0
      IREPN = 0
      DO 48 I=1,N
      IF (IBILL(I,J)-1) 48,5,8
    5 CONTINUE
      IF (IPARTY(I)-1) 48,6,7
    6 IDEMY = IDEMY + 1
      GO TO 48
    7 IREPY = IREPY + 1
      GO TO 48
    8 IF (IBILL(I,J)-2)48,9,48
    9 CONTINUE
      IF (IPARTY(I)-1) 48,10,11
   10 IDEMN = IDEMN + 1
      GO TO 48
   11 IREPN = IREPN + 1
   48 CONTINUE
      JTOTY = IDEMY + IREPY
      JTOTN = IDEMN + IREPN
      TOTDEM = IDEMY + IDEMN
      TOTREP = IREPY + IREPN
      SDEMY = IDEMY
```

```
      SDEMN = IDEMN
      SREPY = IREPY
      SREPN = IREPN
      PPDY = SDEMY/TOTDEM
      PPDN = SDEMN/TOTDEM
      PPRY = SREPY/TOTREP
      PPRN = SREPN/TOTREP
      IF (PPDY-PPDN) 19,20,21
   19 RICED = (PPDN - PPDY) * 100.
      GO TO 25
   20 RICED = 0.0
      GO TO 25
   21 RICED = (PPDY - PPDN) * 100.
   25 CONTINUE
      IF (PPRY-PPRN) 22,23,24
   22 RICER=(PPRN-PPRY)*100
      GO TO 26
   23 RICER = 0.0
      GO TO 26
   24 RICER = (PPRY - PPRN) * 100.
   26 CONTINUE
C CALCULATE THE INDEX OF PARTY LIKENESS
      PDEMY =(SDEMY/TOTDEM) * 100.
      PREPY = (SREPY/TOTREP) * 100.
      IF (PDEMY - PREPY) 81,82,83
   81 PLI = 100. -(PREPY-PDEMY)
      GO TO 84
   82 PLI = 100.
      GO TO 84
   83 PLI = 100. - (PDEMY-PREPY)
   84 CONTINUE
C CALCULATE THE COEFFICIENT OF SIGNIFICANCE
      IF (JTOTN - JTOTY) 71,72,72
   71 RWIN = JTOTY
      QLOSE = JTOTN
      GO TO 73
   72 RWIN = JTOTN
      QLOSE = JTOTY
   73 RVOTE = RWIN + QLOSE
      JVOTE = RVOTE
      JVICMN = JVOTE/2 + 1
      VICMIN=JVICMN
      SIGVAL = SIZE - QLOSE - VICMIN + 2. + ((SIZE - RVOTE + 1.)/(SIZE -
     1QUOR + 2.))
      SIGMAX = 2. + 1./(SIZE - QUOR + 2.)
      JMIN = QUOR/2. + 1.
      QMIN = JMIN
      SIGMIN = SIZE - QMIN + 2. + ((SIZE-QUOR+1.)/(SIZE-QUOR+2.))
  102 COFSIG    = 1. - ((SIGVAL - SIGMAX)/(SIGMIN - SIGMAX))
  103 CONTINUE
C PRINT OUTPUT FOR IBILL(I,J)
      WRITE(61,62) ID,IDEMY,IDEMN,RICED,IREPY,IREPN,RICER,
     3JTOTY,JTOTN,PLI,COFSIG
   62 FORMAT (7X,I4,6X,I4,4X,I4,6X,F6.1,6X,I4,4X,I4,6X,F6.1,6X,I4,5X,I4,
     53X,F4.0,10X,F6.4)
C TEST FOR PUNCH OPTION
      IF (IPUNCH - 1) 105,104,104

  104 PUNCH 63, ID,IDEMY,IDEMN,RICED,IREPY,IREPN,RICER,
     4JTOTY,JTOTN,PLI,COFSIG
   63 FORMAT (I4,2(3X,I3,2X,I3,2X,F6.1),5X,I3,2X,I3,5X,F4.0,2X,F6.4)
  105 ID = ID + 1
      GO TO 1000
 2000 CONTINUE
      STOP
      END
```

FIGURE VIII-3

FORTRAN LANGUAGE LISTING OF VOTES PROGRAM

```
      PROGRAM VOTES
      DIMENSION FMT (12), COFSIG(1000), ID(1000)
C READ FORMAT CARD
      READ (60,1) (FMT(I), I=1,12)
    1 FORMAT (12A6)
      READ (60,2) N, SIZE, QUOR, PUNCH
C READ CONTROL CARD
    2 FORMAT (I4,1X,F4.0,1X,F4.0,5X,F1.0)
      DO 102 I=1,N
C READ DATA ACCORDING TO FORMAT
      READ (60,FMT) ID(I), TOTALY, TOTALN
      IF (TOTALY - TOTALN) 3,4,4
    3 RWIN = TOTALN
      QLOSE = TOTALY
      GO TO 5
    4 RWIN = TOTALY
      QLOSE = TOTALN
    5 CONTINUE
      RVOTE = RWIN + QLOSE
      JVOTE = RVOTE
      JVICMN = JVOTE/2 + 1
      VICMIN = JVICMN
      SIGVAL = SIZE - QLOSE - VICMIN + 2. + ((SIZE - RVOTE + 1.)/(SIZE -
     1QUOR + 2.))
      SIGMAX = 2. + 1./(SIZE - QUOR + 2.)
      IQUOR = QUOR/2. + 1.
      QMIN = IQUOR
      SIGMIN = SIZE - QMIN + 2. + ((SIZE - QUOR + 1.)/(SIZE-QUOR+2.))
  102 COFSIG(I) = 1. - ((SIGVAL - SIGMAX)/(SIGMIN - SIGMAX))
  103 CONTINUE
C THIS COMPLETES COMPUTATIONS.  RANK ORDER SEQUENCE FOLLOWS
      WRITE (61,200)
  200 FORMAT (1H1,5H RANK,5X,8H BILL ID,10X,28H COEFFICIENT OF SIGNIFICA
     6NCE//)
      L = N - 1
      DO 203 K = 1,L
      II = N - K
      DO 203 I = 1,II
      IF (COFSIG(I) - COFSIG(II+1)) 202,203,203
  202 Z = COFSIG(II+1)
      COFSIG(II+1) = COFSIG(I)
      COFSIG(I) = Z
      M = ID(II+1)
      ID(II+1) = ID(I)
      ID(I) = M
  203 CONTINUE
      IRANK = 0
      DO 205 I = 1,N
      IRANK = IRANK + 1
      WRITE (61,204) IRANK, ID(I), COFSIG(I)
  204 FORMAT (1H ,I5,7X,I4,22X,F6.4)
  205 CONTINUE
      IF (PUNCH - 0.) 208,208,206
  206 CONTINUE
      IRANK = 0
      DO 208 I = 1,N
      IRANK = IRANK + 1

      PUNCH 207, ID(I), IRANK, COFSIG(I)
  207 FORMAT (I4,2X,I4,5X,F6.4)
  208 CONTINUE
      STOP
      END
```

CORR: A COMPUTER PROGRAM FOR THE
CROSS-CLASSIFICATION ANALYSIS OF ROLL CALLS

CORR, another Fortran program, is designed to facilitate the cross-classification analysis of legislative roll calls, when party affiliation and vote response are the variables to be analyzed. The results of computations in this routine can be used when the chi-square test or a coefficient of association (phi, lambda, etc.) is desired as a measure of inter-group differences (see Chapter III). The output allows also for the systematic comparison of a series of statistics computed for the same data, and it demonstrates the differential results obtained from the statistics presented in Chapter III. Most of the examples of cross-classification analysis in that chapter were calculated using this program.

The total "yeas" and "nays" for the Democrats and Republicans are read in using the profile cards generated by the ACCUM program, and they are entered in a fourfold table of the following form:

	Yea	Nay
Dems.	a	b
Reps.	c	d

Output consists of the following (for each roll call):

1. A four-fold table of response distributions.

2. The following statistics: chi-square; phi-coefficient; phi-max; the ratio of phi to phi-max; Yule's Q and Y; and lambda ($a,b,$ and ab).

3. The following indexes: Rice Index of Cohesion for each party; Index of Party Likeness.

Figure VIII-4 presents a sample page of output generated by this program.

Figure VIII-4

SAMPLE OUTPUT OF CORR PROGRAM

ANALYSIS OF BILL NO.   1

	YEAS	NAYS	TOTAL
DEMS	32	31	63
REPS	18	15	33
TOTAL	50	46	96

DEMS COHESION =   1.60

ANALYSIS OF BILL NO.   2

	YEAS	NAYS	TOTAL
DEMS	9	48	57
REPS	9	18	27
TOTAL	18	66	84

DEMS COHESION = 68.40

ANALYSIS OF BILL NO.   3

	YEAS	NAYS	TOTAL
DEMS	48	8	56
REPS	19	10	29
TOTAL	67	18	85

DEMS COHESION = 71.40

Order of Cards for Input
 System cards
 Fortran source program
 Input format statement*
 Problem card**
 Data cards

```
   CHISQ =   0.12        YULES Y =  -0.04        YULES Q =  -0.08

   PHI =  -0.04        PHIMAX =   0.75         PHI/PHIMAX =  -0.05

   LAMBDA(A) =   0.00  LAMBDA(B) =   0.00   LAMBDA(AB) =   0.00

REPS COHESION =   9.10            INDEX OF PARTY LIKENESS =   96




   CHISQ =   3.35        YULES Y =  -0.24        YULES Q =  -0.45

   PHI =  -0.20        PHIMAX =   0.76         PHI/PHIMAX =  -0.26

   LAMBDA(A) =   0.00  LAMBDA(B) =   0.00   LAMBDA(AB) =   0.00

REPS COHESION =   0.30            INDEX OF PARTY LIKENESS =   82




   CHISQ =   4.67        YULES Y =   0.28        YULES Q =   0.52

   PHI =   0.23        PHIMAX =   0.72         PHI/PHIMAX =   0.33

   LAMBDA(A) =   0.07  LAMBDA(B) =   0.00   LAMBDA(AB) =   0.04

REPS COHESION =  31.00            INDEX OF PARTY LIKENESS =   80
```

*For this program, the input is the "profile" output of the ACCUM routine. Therefore, the format statement is included in the program. No further preparation is necessary.

**The problem card is punched in the following manner:

Columns
  1-4   blank
  5-8   Number of roll calls for which data is provided. Total
        should be right-adjusted, with leading zeroes punched.
        (Maximum = 9999.)

All other columns should be blank.

Figure VII-5 presents a Fortran listing of the statements
in program CORR that perform the computations resulting in
the output found in Figure VIII-4.

FIGURE VIII-5

FORTRAN LANGUAGE LISTING OF CORR PROGRAM

```
      PROGRAM CORR
    1 CONTINUE
C READ INPUT DATA
      READ(60,300) ID,DEMY,DEMN,RICED,REPY,REPN,RICER,PLI
  300 FORMAT (I4,2(3X,F3.0,2X,F3.0,2X,F6.2),18X,F4.0)
      IF (EOF,60) 203,301
  301 CONTINUE
C DEFINE CELL FREQUENCIES
      A=DEMY $ B=DEMN $ C=REPY $ D=REPN
C DEFINE MARGINALS
      TOTDEM=A+B$TOTREP=C+D$TOTY=A+C$ TOTN=B+D
      EN=TOTDEM+TOTREP
C COMPUTE CHI-SQUARE, PHI-COEFFICIENT
      CHISQ =(EN*(((A*D)-(B*C))**2))/((A+B)*(C+D)*(A+C)*(B+D))
      PHI = ((A*D)-(B*C))/SQRTF((A+B)*(C+D)*(A+C)*(B+D))
C COMPUTE YULES Y, YULES Q
      Y=((SQRTF(A*D)) - (SQRTF(B*C)))/((SQRTF(A*D)) + (SQRTF(B*C)))
      Q=((A*D)-(B*C))/((A*D)+(B*C))
C COMPUTE PHI-MAX
      IF (TOTY-TOTN)10,20,20
   10 ES1 = TOTY $ EL1=TOTN $ GO TO 30
   20 ES1 = TOTN $ EL1 = TOTY
   30 CONTINUE
      IF (TOTDEM - TOTREP)40,50,50
   40 ES2 = TOTDEM $ EL2 = TOTREP $ GO TO 60
   50 ES2 = TOTREP $ EL2 = TOTDEM
   60 CONTINUE            -
      IF (EL1 - EL2) 61,62,62
   61 ELI=EL2 $ SI=ES2 $ ELJ=EL1 $ SJ=ES1
      GO TO 63
   62 ELI=EL1 $ SI=ES1 $ ELJ=EL2 $ SJ=ES2
   63 PHIMAX = SQRTF((SI/ELI) * (ELJ/SJ))
C COMPUTE PHI/PHIMAX (PHIADJ = PHI/PHIMAX)
      PHIADJ = PHI/PHIMAX
C COMPUTE LAMBDA COEFFICIENTS (A,B,AB)
C LAMBDA-A. PREDICT PARTY AFFILIATION FROM VOTING RESPONSE
      IF (A-C) 100,101,101
  100 AMAXJ1=C $ GO TO 120
  101 AMAXJ1=A
  120 CONTINUE
      IF (B-D) 103,104,104
  103 AMAXJ2=D $ GO TO 105
```

```
104 AMAXJ2=B
105 CONTINUE
    IF (TOTDEM - TOTREP) 106,107,107
106 AMAXJ=TOTREP $ GO TO 108
107 AMAXJ=TOTDEM
108 CONTINUE
    ALAMB=(AMAXJ1+AMAXJ2-AMAXJ)/(EN-AMAXJ)
C COMPUTE LAMBDA-B.  PREDICT  RESPONSE FROM PARTY AFFILIATION
    IF (A - B) 109,110,110
109 BMAXK1=B $ GO TO 111
110 BMAXK1=A
111 CONTINUE
    IF (C - D) 112,113,113
112 BMAXK2=D $ GO TO 114
113 BMAXK2=C

114 CONTINUE
    IF (TOTY - TOTN) 115,116,116
115 BMAXK = TOTN $ GO TO 117
116 BMAXK=TOTY
117 CONTINUE
    BLAMB = (BMAXK1+BMAXK2-BMAXK)/(EN-BMAXK)
C COMPUTE LAMBDA-AB
    ABLAMB = (BMAXK1+BMAXK2+AMAXJ1+AMAXJ2-AMAXJ-BMAXK)/((2*EN)-AMAXJ-
    2BMAXK)
C FIX CELL ENTRIES FOR PRINT-OUT
    IDEMY=DEMY $ IDEMN=DEMN $ JTOTD=TOTDEM $ IREPY=REPY $ IREPN=REPN
    JTOTR=TOTREP $ JTOTY=TOTY $ JTOTN=TOTN $ N=EN
    WRITE(61,200) ID,IDEMY,IDEMN,JTOTD,CHISQ,Y, Q,IREPY,IREPN,JTOTR,
    3PHI,PHIMAX,PHIADJ,JTOTY,JTOTN,N,ALAMB,BLAMB,ABLAMB
200 FORMAT (5X,20HANALYSIS OF BILL NO.,I4,///25X,4HYEAS,6X,4HNAYS,6X,
    45HTOTAL//15X,4HDEMS,6X,I4,6X,I4,6X,I4,10X,8HCHISQ = ,F6.2,8X,
    5      10HYULES Y = ,F6.2,6X,10HYULES Q = ,F6.2//15X,4HREPS,6X,I4,
    66X,I4,6X,I4,10X,6HPHI = ,F6.2,7X,  9HPHIMAX = ,F6.2,10X,13HPHI/PHI
    7MAX = ,F6.2///14X,5HTOTAL,6X,I4,6X,I4,6X,I4,10X,12HLAMBDA(A) = ,
    8F6.2,2X,12HLAMBDA(B) = ,F6.2,3X,13HLAMBDA(AB) = ,F6.2//)
    WRITE(61,201) RICED,RICER,PLI
201 FORMAT (20X,16HDEMS COHESION = ,F6.2,10X,16HREPS COHESION = ,F6.2,
    910X,26HINDEX OF PARTY LIKENESS = ,F4.0////)
202 GO TO 1
203 CONTINUE
    STOP
    END
```

AGREE: COMPUTER ROUTINE FOR DERIVING THE RICE-BEYLE INDEX OF COHESION OR THE LIJPHART INDEX OF AGREEMENT FOR EACH PAIR OF VOTERS

The AGREE program provides, for each pair of legislators, a measure of the extent to which they "agree" on a set of votes in the sense of taking similar voting positions. The Index of Agreement is the percentage of times a pair of legislators vote in which each member of the pair votes "yea" or each votes "nay." The Lijphart Index of Agreement is a modification that takes into account the possibility of abstentions (e.g., in the UN). It does this by assigning a value of .5 (partial agreement) to cases in which one legislator abstains and the other votes "yea" or "nay," and a value of 1 when both abstain. These indexes can be used in the determination of categoric group cohesion (see Chapter III) and in the determination of empirically defined blocs (see Chapter IV).

Output consists of the following (for each pair of legislators):

1. An Index of Cohesion or Agreement, depending on values specified on the problem card. (This falls under the column labeled *INDEX*.)
2. The number of total (and partial) agreements (*NAGREE*).
3. The number of votes for which both legislators registered positions. If either or both are absent on a vote, that vote is disregarded in the calculations. (*NTOTAL*).

The value of (2) divided by the value of (3) gives the proportion of agreements. Multiplication by 100 gives the percentage index figure.

Figure VIII-6 presents a sample page of AGREE output.

Order of cards for input:
? System cards
? Source program
· Problem card*
  Input format statement**
  Data cards

*The problem card is punched in the following manner:

Columns

1-5   Sample size, i.e., number of roll calls being processed. Number should be right-adjusted, with leading zeroes punched.

6-10 Number of legislators. Right-adjusted, with leading zeroes punched.

11   Value punched on cards to represent absence.

12   Value punched on cards to represent abstention. When the Index of Cohesion is desired, punch any number not punched on the data cards.

**Variables to be read in format cards (up to 3) are the following:

1. Bill identification number (up to six integers).
2. Roll-call votes.

FIGURE VIII-6
SAMPLE OUTPUT OF AGREE PROGRAM

IDENT	INDEX	NAGREE	NTOTAL
101022-101041	48.87	65.0	133
101022-102041	44.67	67.0	150
101022-102062	75.78	122.0	161
101022-103021	44.78	60.0	134
101022-103062	79.85	107.0	134
101022-104022	73.08	114.0	156
101022-104062	70.53	67.0	95
101022-105041	49.37	78.0	158
101022-106042	77.52	100.0	129
101041-102041	83.22	124.0	149
101041-102062	60.98	100.0	164
101041-103021	83.45	121.0	145
101041-103062	52.27	69.0	132
101041-104022	37.42	58.0	155
101041-104062	40.43	38.0	94
101041-105041	85.71	138.0	161
101041-106042	51.94	67.0	129
102041-102062	57.07	105.0	184
102041-103021	91.30	147.0	161
102041-103062	43.05	65.0	151
102041-104022	28.32	49.0	173
102041-104062	35.79	34.0	95
102041-105041	86.89	159.0	183
102041-106042	50.70	72.0	142
102062-103021	56.47	96.0	170
102062-103062	74.25	124.0	167
102062-104022	67.54	129.0	191
102062-104062	66.98	71.0	106
102062-105041	56.50	113.0	200
102062-106042	77.99	124.0	159
103021-103062	43.07	59.0	137
103021-104022	27.61	45.0	163
103021-104062	32.29	31.0	96
103021-105041	92.90	157.0	169
103021-106042	47.76	64.0	134
103062-104022	77.85	123.0	158
103062-104062	75.28	67.0	89
103062-105041	46.63	76.0	163
103062-106042	78.10	107.0	137
104022-104062	89.32	92.0	103
104022-105041	30.85	58.0	188
104022-106042	72.00	108.0	150
104062-105041	35.92	37.0	103
104062-106042	72.50	58.0	80
105041-106042	50.00	78.0	156

The ID number will be read in using I-format; roll-call votes will be in F-format.

LIMITATIONS

Storage needed should not exceed the capacity of the computer used. Within these limits, the DIMENSION statement can be manipulated to maximize a desired combination (product) of legislators and votes.

Figure VIII-7 presents the Fortran listing for program AGREE.

FIGURE VIII-7

FORTRAN LANGUAGE LISTING OF AGREE PROGRAM

```
      PROGRAM AGREE
      DIMENSION IVAR(30), ID(10), VOT(204,10)
C
C     READING IN CONTROL CARD
      READ(60,50) K, L, ABSENT, ABSTAIN
   50 FORMAT(I5,I5,F1.0,F1.0)
C
C     READING IN THREE VARIABLE FORMAT CARDS
      READ(60,70) (IVAR(I),I=1,30)
   70 FORMAT(10A8)
C
C     READING IN DATA -- IDENTIFICATION AND VOTES
      DO 12 J=1,L
   12 READ(60,IVAR) ID(J), (VOT(I,J), I=1,K)
C
C     MAIN PROGRAM -- LIJPHART#S INDEX OF AGREEMENT
      WRITE(61,300)
  300 FORMAT(1H1,10H       IDENT,9X,5HINDEX,4X,6HNAGREE,3X,6HNTOTAL//)
      L = L-1
      DO 10 I=1,L
      II = I+1
      JJ = I
      DO 10 J=JJ,L
      KDENOM = K
      TOT = 0.0
      DO 8 N=1,K
      IF(VOT(N,I).EQ.ABSENT.OR.VOT(N,II).EQ.ABSENT) 3,4
    3 KDENOM = KDENOM-1
      GO TO 8
    4 IF(VOT(N,I).EQ.VOT(N,II)) 5,6
    5 TOT = TOT+1.0
      GO TO 8
    6 IF(VOT(N,I).EQ.ABSTAIN.AND.VOT(N,II).NE.ABSTAIN.OR.
     1VOT(N,II).EQ.ABSTAIN.AND.VOT(N,I).NE.ABSTAIN) 7,8
    7 TOT = TOT+.5
    8 CONTINUE
      XINDEX = (TOT/KDENOM)*100.0
      WRITE(61,400) ID(I), ID(II), XINDEX, TOT, KDENOM
  400 FORMAT(2X,I6,1H-,I6,4X,F6.2,5X,F5.1,5X,I3)
      II = II+1
   10 CONTINUE
      STOP
      END
```

OTHER PROGRAMS SUITABLE FOR THE ANALYSIS
OF ROLL CALLS

GUTTMAN SCALING

BMDO4S-BMDO8S: This is a set of Guttman scaling programs included in the 1964 edition of *Biomedical Computer Programs*, from the School of Medicine of the University of California at Los Angeles.[7] According to this manual,

> . . . the preprocessor 4S provides data "checking" and provides information for parameters to be specified in the subsequent programs. Program 5S performs the basic Guttman scaling computations and provides a ranking with identification of respondents with scale scores. Program 6S provides initial weighted data for each respondent. Program 7S ranks respondents by the Cornell technique and Program 8S provides final rankings.[8]

The interested reader should refer to the manual for further information.

The IBM 1401 program developed by MacRae for computing a Q coefficient matrix as discussed in Chapter VI is described by D. MacRae, Jr., in "IBM 1401 Q-Matrix and Editing Program for legislative Votes," *Behavioral Science*, 10 (July, 1965), 324.

CROSS-CLASSIFICATION

NUCROS: This program was developed under the supervision of Dr. Kenneth Janda at Northwestern University and is fully described in Chapter VI of *Data Processing: Applications to Political Research*.[9] Several other cross-classification programs are briefly described in the same chapter. A Fortran IV listing of the NUCROS program is included in Appendix C-2 of the same book.

FACTOR ANALYSIS

BMDO3M: General Factor Analysis also is included in the 1964 edition of *Biomedical Computer Programs*. This program computes a principal-components solution and performs an orthogonal rotation according to the varimax criterion. It uses a product-moment correlation coefficient.[10]

MESA 1, programmed by Clarence Bradford at the University of Chicago,* computes a principal-components solution and a varimax orthogonal rotation. It uses a product-moment correlation coefficient[11] and can handle up to one hundred variables. Also, MESA I will provide a complete set of plots for each pair of unrotated factors and for each pair of rotated factors.

MESA 3 has as an interesting feature its ability to handle missing data. It computes a principal-components solution and a varimax orthogonal rotation. Oblique rotation is also possible, with the choice being among the class of analytical solutions called *oblimin*. A product-moment correlation coefficient is used,[12] and the program can analyze a maximum of 236 variables.

TSSA-2 (Test Scorer and Statistical Analysis 2) is a program designed for item analysis. Optional output of the program is a matrix of tetrachoric inter-item correlations and a principal-components factor analysis with orthogonal varimax rotation. It handles up to 120 variables and provides plots for both unrotated and rotated factors. In using this program for item analysis, a *key* card is punched that records the correct response for each item. All one has to do to adapt the program for roll-call analysis is to equate *correct* responses with either *yea* or *nay* responses. It should be noted that this procedure makes absences difficult to handle satisfactorily.[13]

ADDITIONAL SOURCES OF COMPUTER PROGRAMS

Kenneth Janda has described the major sources of computer programs useful in the social sciences in *Data Processing*.[14]

NOTES

[1] For a discussion of preliminary procedures in collecting and coding roll-call data see Kenneth Janda, *Data Processing: Applications to Political Research*. (Evanston, Ill.: Northwestern University Press, 1965), pp. 29-33.

[2] The reader is referred to Janda, *op. cit.*, for a presentation of electronic processing techniques aimed specifically at the political scientist. For relevant information on computer language, the following Fortran instructions books may be useful: Elliott I. Organ-

ick, *A Fortran Primer* (Reading, Mass.: Addison-Wesley Publishing Company, 1963); and Daniel D. McCracken, *A Guide to FORTRAN Programming* (New York: John Wiley and Sons, Inc., 1961). The manufacturers of electronic data-processing equipment, such as IBM and the Control Data Corporation, have specialized manuals for users of their machines. These manuals can be obtained directly from the companies themselves, if not available otherwise.

³ For further information about the ACCUM, VOTES, or CORR programs, the reader may contact Meredith W. Watts, Department of Political Science, Northwestern University, Evanston, Illinois. For information on the AGREE program, contact Allen R. Wilcox at the same institution.

In particular, the Fortran statements that cause the machine to "read" and "write" information (input and output statements) should be checked for compatibility on the user's equipment. Although each of these programs has been thoroughly tested and found satisfactory on the Northwestern University system, we assume no responsibility for their operation on other systems.

The first point to be remembered in transcribing these statements is that each must be punched in columns 7-72 of their respective cards. Columns 1-5 are used for the numbers that precede certain statements. Any number in column 6 indicates that the statement is a continuation or completion of a preceding card. Cards beginning with a *C* in the first column are "COMMENT" cards, which include information to help the user identify segments of the program and are not necessary to execution. Finally, columns 73-80 (not reproduced here) may be used to label the statement so that the cards may be kept in order by the programmer. With this minimum information, the user can punch the statements on cards; a more detailed presentation of programming conventions may be found in the Fortran texts cited above.

⁴ Stuart Rice, *Quantitative Methods in Politics* (New York: Alfred A. Knopf, 1928).

⁵ *Ibid.*

⁶ See William H. Riker, "A Method for Determining the Significance of Roll Calls in Voting Books," in John Wahlke and Heinz Eulau (eds.), *Legislative Behavior* (Glencoe, Ill.: The Free Press, 1959), pp. 377-84.

⁷ W. J. Dixon (ed.), *BMD:Biomedical Computer Programs* (Los Angeles: UCLA School of Medicine, Department of Preventive Medicine and Public Health, Health Sciences Computing Facility, 1964). Copies of the BMD manual may be purchased at $5.00 each (postpaid) from the UCLA Student Store, 308 Westwood Boulevard, Los Angeles, California 90024.

⁸ *Ibid.*, p. 311.

[9] See note 1.

[10] Within the range of this computer program it should be possible to use correlation measures other than the Pearson product-moment coefficients specified. When the data are categorized as "1" (yea) and '0" (nay) for the set of roll-call responses, the computer will calculate a phi-coefficient, the functional equivalent for the Pearson *r* when the data are dichotomized.

If the researcher wishes to follow the example of factor analysis used in Chapter VII of this book and rank his responses in polytomous fashion ($+1,0,-1$), the computer will generate a statistic that is similar to the Spearman rank-order correlation coefficient (r_s).

In both these cases, the manner in which the roll-call responses are categorized will alter the nature and interpretation of the correlation coefficient that is produced by the computer.

[11] See note 10.

[12] See note 10.

[13] Write-ups and binary decks for MESA 1, MESA 3, and TSSA-2 are available at the Northwestern University Computing Center.

[14] Janda, *op. cit.*, pp. 116-17.

AUTHOR INDEX

SUBJECT INDEX